Burlington

Buffalo

Albany

New York

Omaha

Chicago

Cleveland

MW01041461

Also by Dayton Duncan

Out West: A Journey Through Lewis and Clark's America
Lewis & Clark: The Journey of the Corps of Discovery (with Ken Burns)
Grass Roots
Miles from Nowhere: Tales from America's Contemporary Frontier
People of the West
The West: An Illustrated History for Children
Mark Twain (with Geoffrey C. Ward and Ken Burns)

Also by Ken Burns

Lewis & Clark: The Journey of the Corps of Discovery (with Dayton Duncan)
Baseball: An Illustrated History (with Geoffrey C. Ward)
The Shakers: Hands to Work, Hearts to God (with Amy S. Burns)
The Civil War: An Illustrated History (with Geoffrey C. Ward and Ric Burns)
Not for Ourselves Alone: The Story of Elizabeth Cady Stanton and Susan B. Anthony (with Geoffrey C. Ward)
Jazz: A History of America's Music (with Geoffrey C. Ward)
Mark Twain (with Geoffrey C. Ward and Dayton Duncan)

➤   ➤   ➤   ➤   ➤   ➤   ➤   ➤   ➤   ➤   ➤   ➤   ➤   ➤   ➤   ➤   ➤   ➤

HORATIO'S DRIVE

BY **Dayton Duncan**

BASED ON A
DOCUMENTARY FILM
DIRECTED BY **Ken Burns**

WRITTEN BY
Dayton Duncan
WITH A PREFACE
BY **Ken Burns**

PICTURE RESEARCH BY
**Susanna Steisel,
Jennifer Stanelle** AND
Pam Tubridy Baucom

ALFRED A. KNOPF
NEW YORK
2003

HORATIO'S
DRIVE
AMERICA'S FIRST
ROAD TRIP

FOR OUR FATHERS, DUDLEY DUNCAN AND ROBERT K. BURNS, JR.

This Is a Borzoi Book Published by Alfred A. Knopf

Copyright © 2003 by The American Lives II Film Project, LLC

All rights reserved under International and Pan-American Copyright Conventions. Published in the United States by Alfred A. Knopf, a division of Random House, Inc., New York, and simultaneously in Canada by Random House of Canada Limited, Toronto. Distributed by Random House, Inc., New York.

www.aaknopf.com

Knopf, Borzoi Books, and the colophon are registered trademarks of Random House, Inc.

Library of Congress Cataloging-in-Publication Data

Duncan, Dayton.
    Horatio's drive / by Dayton Duncan and Ken Burns.— 1st ed.
        p.   cm.
    Companion volume to the PBS documentary of the same title.
    ISBN 0-375-41536-X
    1. United States—Description and travel. 2. Jackson, Horatio Nelson, b. 1862—Journeys—United States. 3. Automobile travel—United States—History—20th century. 4. Duncan, Dayton—Journeys—United States. I. Burns, Ken, 1953– II. Horatio's drive (Television program) III. Title.
    E168 .D88 2003
    917.304911—dc21
                                                            2002035736

Manufactured in the United States of America

First Edition

CONTENTS

A Walpole Roa

THE WAY WE ENTER OUR HISTORY

I love to drive. I *love* to drive. I can think of only a few pleasures in life that are more satisfying than getting in a car and starting out on a road trip. Especially if it's new territory. I love realizing—and it is a constant and sustaining realization—that I am on a road I've never been on before, that what I am seeing unfolding before me is brand new, and it is only a short leap in my mind before I start thinking about who were the first Europeans to see this exact view and what they thought, and then it is an even shorter leap and I am trying to imagine what this looked like to Native Americans: a pristine, unspoiled Nature ready to accept silently whatever those contradictory and ambiguous humans would do to it over succeeding ages. In those moments, it seems as if it could be possible to comprehend the entire United States, to know it—this beautiful, fragile land—like one knows a familiar and beloved poem; that if one just kept on the road, kept going down new highways, it would be pos-

sible not only to express in words but to actually experience, to apprehend in scope, as perhaps a single blood cell does the whole body, this country I love so much.

Such are the dreams of the road, and while I am perfectly content to do all of this alone—and have, in good times and bad—there is something about sharing the journey that magnifies and intensifies all of those thoughts and vistas. An unforgettable trip along the Skyline Drive in the Blue Ridge Mountains with my usually distracted father when I was five (and its equally memorable complement forty-two years later with my then fourteen-year-old youngest daughter) comes to mind, as does the slightly sad image of my family, including my desperately sick mother, packed into a huge rented station wagon, groaning under the weight of everything we could not bear to entrust to movers, taking our worries and hopes from Newark, Delaware, to Ann Arbor, Michigan, when I was nearly ten. I recall a trip to an utterly exotic Florida complete with a dramatic tire blow-out and exquisite pauses to chase armadillos through the "jungle," and an all-nighter with other hippies to an antiwar march in Washington, D.C., when I almost choked to death on a lemon drop on the Ohio Turnpike and won fifteen dollars at bingo to the chagrin of the regular patrons at the Volunteer Fire Department of Pikesville, Maryland.

Filming a 1903 Winton

logical station at Mountain Lake, Virginia, where my brother and I would be parked with relatives, and my father made up, on the spot, what seemed like dozens of hilarious, nonsensical verses to a blues tune he titled "Twenty Miles From Athens" (Ohio). And then there was a more recent trip through a very long night from Michigan with my father's ashes and memorabilia from his disappointing, truncated life

I have an almost perfect memory of every route and approach we have taken over the last thirteen straight summers as my daughters and I headed to the Telluride Film Festival in the majestic and breathtaking San Juan Mountains of Colorado. I can remember as if it were yesterday a trip we took back from Massachusetts at age nine when I looked out the window and counted under my breath to eight thousand or something equally ridiculous, and the time after my mother died when we survivors drove to the bio-

slowing me down, my aloneness mitigated by friends and loved ones who gently urged me onward with perfectly timed cell-phone calls.

But it is the trips I have taken with my dear friend and colleague Dayton Duncan that have meant the most to me over the years and have brought me the most sustained joy and happy memories that I can summon from the road. I first "met" Dayton fifteen years ago on a road trip I had yet to take. We had been then just casual acquaintances when he shared with me his remarkable first book, *Out West,* in which he retraced and retold Lewis and Clark's stunning and heroic journey in humorous and unusually moving ways. I loved the book. It was eloquent and generous and spoke to a part in me, as yet unarticulated, that yearned for more experiences of the road. In the highest compliment I can give, no one loves his country more than Dayton and it is a love tested along hundreds of thousands of miles of roads in the blood system of America. Reading his book and discovering that we shared many other common interests and enthusiasms propelled us into a friendship I treasure as much as any other and launched a completely satisfying professional association that has produced over the last dozen years several films and companion books, including *The West, Mark Twain,* and of course *Lewis and Clark: The Journey of the Corps of Discovery.* Discovery, indeed.

That film (and book) project took us again and again to nearly every spot along the Lewis and Clark trail as we strained to see and record what the earlier explorers had experienced. Traveling along steep mountain roads or the dirt tracks of the prairie in our trusty Suburban, our friendship deepened. It was clear that we both loved maps and navigating and doing the driving, and while I cannot speak for Dayton, I know now that he is one of the few people I trust unhesitatingly behind the wheel. We both loved to get up early, to "steal a march" on some remote location, or shot, or sunset, and sometime, I'm not sure exactly when, during that earlier production we began to play a game with each other. Mindful of the rather limited cuisine at the local cafés of the dozens of small towns we passed through, one of us, just before lunch or supper, would ask the other, "What are you planning to eat once we get into (say) Geraldine, Montana?" (At that point, the town would be just visible off in the distance maybe ten miles away.) With a straight face, the other would launch into the most elaborate description of the most amazing multicourse gourmet meal this side of Paris, France, at which point, the other would say simply, "So, what do you want on your cheeseburger?" Then, we would silently drive the rest of the way into Geraldine (or such like town) and have . . . a cheeseburger.

As I took more road trips with Dayton—for the Lewis and Clark film and other projects—an old Spanish proverb would come to mind that the late, great animation genius Chuck Jones had once told me. "It's not the inn at the end of the day," he said, "but the road." Like the country Dayton and I both love, dedicated to a *pursuit* of happiness, always in the process of *becoming,* the open road, leading us onward, was the perfect metaphor for our own personal and collective search. Somewhere out there, we would find out something about our country and ourselves, and like Lewis and Clark, it would always be for us a journey of discovery.

And somewhere along that road, in the American West, in the mid-1990s (though Dayton insists he told me years before in 1990), I began to realize that he was trying to interest me in making a film on the story of Horatio Nelson Jackson. It was the little-known story of the first cross-country automobile trip, accomplished with exquisite historical symmetry, he regaled me, exactly one hundred years after Meriwether Lewis got his marching orders from Thomas Jefferson to find out what the fifteen million dollars he'd spent for the Louisiana Territory had bought.

Jackson's trip had been made "on a dare, a fifty dollar bet," Dayton said, "in a men's club in San Francisco, when in front of Jackson, some gentlemen had pooh-poohed the future of the horseless carriage." Jackson had had almost no automotive experience, Dayton continued, and yet he was going to try to do what many automotive experts had tried and failed miserably to do: to drive all the way to New York City in less than ninety days. The story, he said, had everything. It was about freedom, good old American perseverance, the open road; there was humor and the overcoming of obstacles, and because others joined the quest, it was like a race, too, and it showed the country, all of it, on the cusp of extraordinary change.

At first, I have to admit I wasn't that impressed. I didn't yet see a film in it, and I was distracted by several other projects that were demanding all of my attention. But over the years, Dayton continued to champion doing a film and book on what he now called "Horatio's Drive," and he began to dig even more: tracing Jackson's exact route on maps; contacting local historical societies and newspapers in the little western towns along the way, where Jackson's trip had stirred up so much excitement and curiosity; and following the trail in Vermont, where Jackson had lived, turning up some tantalizing newspaper clippings and a treasure trove of nearly one hundred snapshots Jackson had taken along the way. He visited the Smithsonian in Washington, where the car is still on display, and found a scrapbook filled with newspaper accounts of the journey. At each step, I was impressed with Dayton's dogged determination (not too dissimilar from Jackson's own marvelous optimism), but still not quite sure he had amassed the critical mass to turn this fascinating story into a film and book. Dayton was adamant, however, and so I finally agreed (I trusted him implicitly) and we started to move forward on the project.

Although we would like to believe that our films (and their companion books) offer a fresh and dramatic perspective on the subjects we take on, they rarely break new scholarly ground, offer up new facts unknown to specialists in the field, or do original research. We are content, under the watchful eyes of our historical advisors, to arrange and re-arrange existing materials in an artful and dramatic fash-

Filming in Wyoming

ion that we hope a national public television audience and general readers will find compelling. But because of Dayton Duncan and his wife Dianne's stubborn perseverance, *Horatio's Drive* will feature new research and add significantly to future understanding of the trip.

Checking obituaries, death certificates, and funeral records for possible descendants, and making literally hundreds of "cold calls," Dianne was able to track down two grand-daughters of Jackson's, who not only generously agreed to

share memories of their grandfather with us on film, but produced heretofore unpublished letters and tele-grams that Jackson had sent back from most of his stops along the way, detailing nearly every moment of his arduous, hilarious, historic, clearly impressive road trip. The letters helped to fill in huge gaps in the story and to settle discrepancies that had cropped up in conflicting newspaper accounts. But most of all, they made Horatio Nelson Jackson come alive as never before. He was a real person now, and now we had a real film. (A little later, Tom Hanks would agree to read, off-camera, Horatio's words for our film, and together with a superb supporting cast reading a chorus of other first-person accounts, we felt at times as if we were actually *there* with Jackson.)

Armed with Dayton's script, which forms the backbone of this book, we set out to retrace Horatio's drive just as we sought to evoke, with live modern cinematography, Lewis and Clark's progress on that earlier project. We ended up covering more than ten thousand miles—nearly twice as many miles as Jackson— because we had to search back and forth for those dirt tracks and old trails that resembled the nearly impossible conditions Jackson faced at every bend in the road.

During our expeditions, we went up rocky mountain trails, forded any number of streams and creeks, drove through orchards and alkali flats, went careering down red rock canyons, and bumped along railroad tracks—just like Horatio Nelson Jackson. We chased the massive terrifying storms that still patrol the prairies, just as we are sure Jackson tried to avoid or outrun them. We stood in awe in front of an old Pony Express way station that Jackson passed a century earlier, and one late afternoon in southwestern Wyoming we filmed along a dirt track that was at once a

Filming on the move

part of the Oregon, California, Pony Express, *and* Mormon Trails.

Not far from that spot, we, like Jackson, got lost. We didn't go without food for thirty-six hours, as Jackson did, but after eating too big a meal at Cruel Jack's, a truck stop near Rock Springs, a few of us might have wanted to. Once, coming into Chicago, where three major interstates converge, we saw more cars in an hour's time than the number of cars that existed in America in 1903, the year Horatio made his impulsive trip.

We outfitted our wonderful cinematographer Allen Moore with a canvas harness and strapped him to the hood of our Chevy Suburban so that the filming would not just have the painterly style of our previous work, but the visceral, sometimes gut-wrenching perspective that Horatio and his companions surely had. (Later, we would "distress" this footage to give it just the right look we wanted, to give viewers a sense of what it must have been like on the road back then.) In the Cascade Mountains of northern California, two Indians watched in amazement as we charged a mountain stream, Allen mounted on the front, just a few feet from a perfectly good bridge. Near Farson, Wyoming, a ranch hand watched Allen put his bra-like harness on for a drive near the historic South Pass, and then turned to his cowboy friend and said, "I'll be getting free drinks at the bar for a month for telling this story."

Along the route, we stopped at country museums, modest libraries, and proud historical societies in many of the small towns Jackson had passed through and found even more great photos: some of Horatio we never knew existed, and some of town life at the turn of the twentieth century that helped us immeasurably in conjuring up that earlier era and the excitement townspeople obviously felt at his arrival. Newspaper morgues in those same small towns added many colorful local accounts that we hadn't known about.

Through it all, we could not help but drink up the powerful tonic, the powerful medicine, which moving across this extraordinary country always is. It sustained and inspired and overwhelmed us. We felt often as if we were moving through time as well as through the landscape, and came to understand, as no armchair surveyor ever can, the immense size

and almost stupefying distance that is the American West, both today and yesterday, when Horatio Nelson Jackson made his bold, and now to us almost unbelievable, run.

In an interview for our film on Mark Twain, the novelist Russell Banks said that despite our common "threads of history" with Europe, we Americans have had to write our own epics, our own *Iliads* and *Odysseys*, that illuminate the differences between us and our European forebears. And the elements, he said, "that make us different are essentially two: race and space." As filmmakers who have been interested in learning ever more about the mechanics of our complicated and often dysfunctional republic, we have returned again and again to the question of race in many of our films, trying to come to terms with the monumental hypocrisy born at our inception when our founders attempted to reconcile chattel slavery in a new nation that had just proclaimed the universal rights of all men.

But we have also been equally drawn over the years to the power and magnetism of the American landscape, this huge space of ours, and its central role in the formation of a distinct American sensibility and character. It, too, has figured in some way in nearly every film we have made. Sometimes, as in *The West, Lewis & Clark,* and *Mark Twain,* Banks' twin themes intertwine and commingle in almost equal and obvious measure. (In other films, these themes are somewhat distinct, though the fact that race may have been dominant in *The Civil War, Baseball,* and *Jazz* did not mean that the question of space wasn't always close by, continually influencing the American narrative we sought to explore.)

In *Horatio's Drive,* we have tried to paint a seemingly simpler story, one of history from the bottom up, not top down, but one that gets its energy from the sheer physicality of these United States and the extraordinary human beings who have inhabited that space. The virtues and qualities and strengths that we hope radiate out from this story are seemingly simpler, too, though, as Dayton Duncan knows in his gut, the medicinal force of a great road trip, like the horseless carriage or this still wild American landscape itself, cannot be dismissed.

Maybe, William Least Heat-Moon, author of the magnificent *Blue Highways* and a commentator in this film, put it best:

There's nothing that we can do that is more American than getting in a car and striking out across country. I think as a nation we can think of few things that draw us more strongly than a piece of roadway heading we know not where. This is the way we grow up, this is the way we enter our history: get in a car and find the country.

And ourselves.

KEN BURNS
Walpole, New Hampshire

A country lane in Walpole, New Hampshire ➤

CHAPTER ONE

A PASSING MECHANICAL FANCY

On the evening of May 19, 1903, in the University Club in San Francisco, a group of well-to-do men were sharing drinks and conversation. The talk centered on President Theodore Roosevelt's political fortunes, recent flooding along the Mississippi River, and the chances that the Boston Pilgrims might take the pennant in the brand-new American League. Then the discussion turned to another topic: the future of a new machine that only recently had been showing up on the streets of major American cities—the automobile.

Horatio Nelson Jackson, a guest at the club and one of the participants in the ensuing debate, suddenly found himself completely outnumbered. "The majority opinion," he would later recall, "was that save for short distances the automobile was an unreliable novelty, a passing mechanical fancy which thinking men could do no other than discard, as the horse continued to demonstrate his

The University Club

proper place as the dependable servant of mankind for travel."

Jackson was a thirty-one-year-old doctor from Burlington, Vermont. Three years earlier, after a mild case of tuberculosis, he had given up his medical practice, but he was still energetic and brimming with new ideas. He had just been to Mexico and Alaska to pursue investments in gold and silver mines, and on the way back home he had stopped off in California to purchase two automobiles and learn how to drive them before shipping them to

Vermont by rail. "I had been something of a horse-fancier, owning a small stable of thoroughbreds," Jackson remembered, "but I had succumbed completely to a primary enthusiasm for the newfangled horseless buggy."

That evening at the University Club, Jackson argued that the automobile was more than a "rich man's toy" suitable only for short drives on city boulevards, and he disagreed when the other men declared that a car could never make it all the way across the country. "Everyone," he said, "pooh-poohed the idea of even attempting such a journey."

Someone wagered fifty dollars that no one could drive to New York City in less than three months.

Jackson immediately accepted the challenge.

Only four days later, he would set off from San Francisco intending to win the bet—and make history along the way.

At the time, the odds were heavily stacked against Jackson reaching his destination.

As a means of travel, automobiles were still in their infancy in 1903. Only ten years earlier, two bicycle mechanics in Springfield, Massachusetts, Charles E. and J. Frank Duryea, had started making what they called gasoline-powered "motor wagons"—the first American automobiles. (Germany's Karl Benz is generally credited with creating the world's first automobile, in 1886.) Other entrepreneurs quickly followed suit. A young machinist and self-taught engineer in Detroit named Henry Ford produced a "Quadricycle," a machine that weighed only five hundred pounds and could reach the unheard-of speed of twenty miles per hour. In Lansing, Michigan, Ransom Olds made a motor carriage that was better than a horse, he said, because "it never kicks or bites, never tires on long runs, . . . never sweats in hot weather . . . and eats only while on the road."

In those early years, electric-powered vehicles were as common as the "petrocars" that used gasoline, or the "steamers" produced by the Stanley brothers of Massachusetts, which required twenty minutes in order for their boilers to heat up enough water to get things moving.

Kerosene-burning vehicle, 1884

Bollee tricar, 1900

Boston police with Stanley Steamer

Duryea in Springfield, Massachusetts

Electric taxi, New York City

Stanhope electric car

On some vehicles the steering wheel was on the left; on others, the right (left-hand drive would become standard in American cars around 1908). Many had no steering wheel at all, using a tiller or levers to guide the horseless carriage down the street. Some had metal poles mounted underneath that could be dropped like anchors, nailing the car to the road if it started to slide sideways or roll backwards down a hill. Drivers were called "motorists," "chauffeurs"—and, as the European term "automobile" slowly took root, "automobilists."

Automobiles were beyond most people's financial reach—ranging in price from $650 to more than $6,000, while the average American earned less than $500 a year. Car ownership was limited to the small number of wealthy buyers—doctors, businessmen, millionaires—who could afford the purchase price and who also often hired a factory representative to arrive with their new car for a week or more of personal lessons in the bewilderingly new intricacies of handling an automobile.

For many Americans, automobiles were not only too expensive, they were downright dangerous. In cities all around the nation, residents began complaining about the noise of the new machines, the clouds of dust they raised while whirling through town, and the threat they posed

Locomobile at Yosemite, 1900

A steam-powered stage

Verse 1

Johnny O'Connor bought an automobile,
He took his sweetheart for a ride one Sunday,
Johnny was togged up in his best Sunday clothes,
She nestled close to his side.
Things went just dandy 'till he got down the road,
Then something happened to the old machinery,
That engine got his goat, off went his hat and coat,
   Everything needed repairs.

Verse 2

Millionaire Wilson said to Johnny one day,
Your little sweetheart don't appreciate you,
I have a daughter who is hungry for love,
She likes to ride by the way.
Johnny had visions of a million in gold,
He took her riding in his little auto,
But every time that he went to say "marry me,"
   'Twas the old story again.

Chorus

He'd have to get under, get out and get under
To fix his little machine,
He was just dying to cuddle his queen,
But ev'ry minute, when he'd begin it,
He'd have to get under, get out and get under,
Then he'd get back at the wheel.
A dozen times they'd start to hug and kiss
And then the darned old engine it would miss
And then he'd have to get under, get out and get under
And fix up his automobile.

Music by Maurice Abrahams
Words by Grant Clarke and Edgar Leslie

Romance and cars: hand in hand from the start ➤

to horse-drawn carriages, bicyclists, and pedestrians. (The nation's first fatality from a car accident occurred on September 13, 1899, when Henry H. Bliss stepped off a streetcar at Seventy-fourth Street and Central Park West in Manhattan and was run over by an electric-powered taxicab.) Vermont enacted a law, based on an English statute, stating that every auto had to be preceded down the street by an adult waving a red flag. Tennessee required motorists to post a week's notice before starting out on any trip. In Glencoe, Illinois, someone stretched a steel cable across the road to stop what they called the "devil wagons." Some cities banned automobiles altogether.

By the end of the nineteenth century, there were only eight thousand cars in the United States compared to 14

First transcontinental attempt: the Davises, 1899

million horses. Blacksmiths outnumbered doctors. And most Americans rarely traveled farther than twelve miles from their home—the distance a horse-and-wagon could take them from home and back in a day. If they wished to

A blacksmith contemplates his future.

go any greater distance, they had to go by rail, restricting themselves to the railroad's schedule and the confinement of its passenger cars.

But to a small number of Americans, the automobile offered new possibilities for the two things they cherished most: mobility and freedom. To them, the automobile represented the future, destined someday to make both the horse *and* the railroad obsolete. It wasn't long before a few of them decided to dramatize their point by trying to drive all the way across the country.

In the summer of 1899, a mechanic named John D. Davis and his wife, journalist Louise Hitchcock Davis, motored their 7-horsepower Duryea out of New York City on the first-known attempt to drive a car across the continent—a highly publicized event underwritten by two newspapers and an automobile company anxious to prove that American cars were superior to French and English machines. They expected to reach San Francisco in a month.

They're Off.

Almost immediately, everything went wrong. Parts broke. A rear wheel collapsed. And the Davises' progress was so slow and torturous that a one-armed bicyclist, who had left New York ten days after their departure, passed them before they reached Syracuse. Three months later, after hobbling into Chicago, the couple gave up their journey altogether. The automobile, a discouraged Louise Davis wrote, "is a treacherous animal for a long trip."

Two years after the Davises' failure, Alexander Winton made the next transcontinental attempt. Winton was one of the nation's leading car manufacturers (the one hundred vehicles his company produced in 1899 had also made it the nation's largest), a renowned innovator in design and production, and a holder of several speed and endurance records (he had earlier won national fame by driving from Cleveland to New York). For this trip he decided to drive from west to east, in order to conquer the hardest part of the journey first, when his car would be at its best. "If

Second attempt: Alexander Winton, 1901

May 20, 1901, planning to reach New York City in two months. With Winton himself attending to the necessary repairs whenever the car broke down, they made good time surmounting the Sierra Nevada and were soon crossing the deserts of Nevada. But on the tenth day of the trip, a mere 530 miles from their starting point in San Francisco, the car became stuck in a sand drift and Winton called an abrupt end to his journey. "This automobile has taken more abuse and hard service than any machine ever stood," he bragged of the car his company had made, "but with all her power it is utterly impossible to drive through this sand. A Winton motor carriage cannot be expected to work a miracle."

———————————

success in this endeavor is possible," the *Motor Vehicle Review* promised, "Mr. Winton will surely achieve it."

Accompanied by his full-time publicity agent, Charles B. Shanks, Winton left San Francisco to great fanfare on

Horatio Nelson Jackson, 1903

Horatio Nelson Jackson, the next person to try in 1903, seemed even less likely to succeed. He lacked any corporate backing or publicity, knew next to nothing about the mechanics of automobiles, and had done little or no planning. But in his quest to do what no one else had ever accomplished, Jackson possessed two important qualities that would prove invaluable—an indomitable spirit, fired by his newfound enthusiasm for the horseless carriage; and deep pockets, thanks to his wife's inherited fortune.

Jackson himself came from relatively modest means. A minister's son, born in 1872, he had earned his medical degree at the University of Vermont in 1893 and practiced for a few years in the towns of Brattleboro and Burlington. Then, in 1899, he married Bertha Richardson Wells, the daughter of one of the richest men in Vermont, the founder of Paine's Celery Compound, a popular cure-all that was 20 percent grain alcohol. It was her money that allowed the newlyweds to make an extended tour of Europe, buy Providence Island in Lake Champlain for a summer residence, invest in mining opportunities, purchase race horses and then automobiles—all despite Jackson's having given up his medical practice. And it would be her money financing his improbable journey across the nation. Bertha (whom Jackson affectionately called "Swipes" for reasons forever lost to history) supported his decision to make the trip, but thought it best to return home by passenger train instead of accompanying her husband.

In her place, Jackson hired Sewall K. Crocker, a twenty-two-year-old former professional bicycle racer from Tacoma, Washington, who was working in California as a mechanic in a gasoline-engine factory. Crocker may also have been giving Jackson and his wife private driving lessons on the two automobiles they had recently purchased and already shipped back to Vermont.

For the arduous trip they were now about to attempt, Crocker strongly advised buying one of the touring cars produced by Alexander Winton's company in Cleveland—the sturdiest and most reliable automobile being made, in his estimation. "It will carry you through if anything will," he told Jackson. But no new ones could be found on the Pacific Coast. (The Winton Motor Carriage Company would make a grand total of 850 cars in 1903, part of the roughly 11,000 autos manufactured in the

Bertha "Swipes" Jackson

United States that year, bringing the nation's total car registration to 33,000. Most new cars—especially top-of-the-line vehicles like the Winton—were preordered from the manufacturer rather than purchased at a dealership.)

After a quick but persistent search, Jackson at last found a Wells, Fargo executive in San Francisco willing to part with a 1903 Winton— but only for a $500 bonus over the list price of $2,500, even though the car already had nearly a thousand miles on it and both rear tires were already in poor condition. Jackson gladly paid the $3,000 and immediately went to work with Crocker on preparing the car for the journey.

The Winton had a two-cylinder, 20-horsepower engine directly underneath the driver's seat, with a chain drive, capable of speeds up to thirty miles per hour; two speeds forward and one reverse; steering wheel on the right; no windshield and no top. It featured two of Alexander Winton's many engineering innovations: a ratcheted lever that

Through all the Crush with Perfect Ease

An accomplishment possible only in an automobile so simple and sensitive, in its control and steering mechanism, that it responds like a living thing to the driver's wishes. That automobile is the

Winton

Absolute control of the car is assured by the Winton method of motor government which is simplicity itself. A little spring button under the driver's right foot operates the air governor, which controls the speed of the motor. When the pressure upon this button is increased the motor speeds up and the car forges ahead. Release the pressure, the motor slows down and the car speed diminishes. You get any desired variation by the use of this throttle button. The method is so simple and effective that the driver increases or decreases speed of car without conscious effort. There is no automobile manufactured or sold in America which combines so many features of real excellence. The Winton is a practical result of long experience thoroughly tried out. It is of clever design, beautifully finished, and the entire correctness of our horizontal, double opposed cylinder motor is being demonstrated daily to the complete satisfaction of the very best mechanical minds.

The price of this superb 20 horse-power car complete with detachable tonneau, full brass side lamps, tools, etc., is $2,500.00.

Visit any of our branch or agency depots in all leading cities, and the features of Winton excellence will be demonstrated.

THE WINTON MOTOR CARRIAGE CO.,
Berea Road, Cleveland, U. S. A.

prevented broken arms if the engine unexpectedly back-fired in the midst of being crank-started; and a hinge that allowed the steering wheel to be tipped away as the driver took his position. Leather-upholstered seats were mounted high on a wooden body painted a reddish maroon with, as the sales brochure promised, "just enough polished brass . . . to enliven the general effect."

Crocker removed the tonneau (backseat) to make room for the piles of equipment Jackson quickly purchased: sleeping bags and cooking gear; rubber mackintoshes for themselves and even one that covered the entire car; coats and sweaters and two telescope valises for their clothing; a set of tools, including two jacks, a spade, and a fireman's axe; a block and tackle with 150 feet of hemp rope; fishing gear; a shotgun, rifle, pistols, and ammunition—and a small Kodak camera to record his trip. With Jackson (225 pounds) and Crocker (150 pounds) on board, the fully loaded vehicle weighed more than a ton and a half.

There were no gas stations at the time (the first would appear in St. Louis in 1905), but general stores in most towns carried fuel for farm machinery, stoves, and water pumps. The Winton's gas tank held between eleven and twelve gallons, "sufficient to run the car about 175 miles over ordinary roads," according to the company's sales

Crocker fine tunes the **Vermont**

Crocker at the wheel

brochure. Jackson strapped on additional tanks to carry five gallons of cylinder oil and twelve extra gallons of gasoline, in case of an emergency. Unable to locate new tires for the worn pair on the rear wheels, he hoped the single spare he brought along would suffice if one of them gave out.

According to the Winton Company's numbering system, the car Jackson had purchased was No. 1684, but its new owner concluded that a machine entrusted with so much needed a name, not a number. Like many automobile owners who would follow him, Jackson already was thinking of his new car as if it had a personality of its own, despite the injunction printed clearly in the Winton's instruction manual. "Remember," it said, "that an automobile has no brains. You must do its thinking. It is merely a man-made machine, subject to man's control, and under thoughtful handling, will perform all the work for which it is designed."

In honor of the state where he and Bertha made their home, the place he hoped Winton No. 1684 would eventually deliver him in triumph, Jackson officially christened his vehicle the *Vermont*. With that, a mere four days after making his impulsive wager, he was ready to go.

Winton No. 1684: the **Vermont** ➤

CHAPTER TWO

THE HARDEST WORK I EVER DID

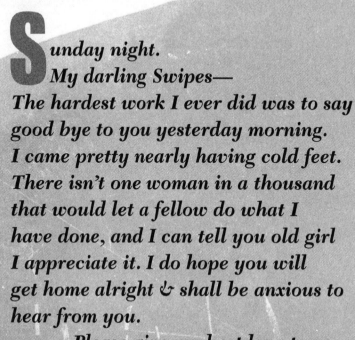

Sunday night.
My darling Swipes—
The hardest work I ever did was to say good bye to you yesterday morning. I came pretty nearly having cold feet. There isn't one woman in a thousand that would let a fellow do what I have done, and I can tell you old girl I appreciate it. I do hope you will get home alright & shall be anxious to hear from you.

. . . Please give my best love to your mother & tell [my] father & mother that I love them as much as ever. I shall write you when I can & shall depend on you to keep them posted.

Yours till New York, Nelson.

Take good care of yourself & don't worry.

After seeing his wife off at San Francisco's railroad station on Saturday morning, May 23, 1903, Jackson joined Crocker in the early afternoon at the Palace Hotel, and the two of them set off in the *Vermont* for their long journey east. They crossed the bay on the Oakland ferry and made good time through the town of Hayward. But only fifteen miles into their trip, a rear tire blew. Crocker replaced it with the only spare they had, and they motored on to Tracy for the night, having covered eighty-three miles for the day, according to the car's cyclometer.

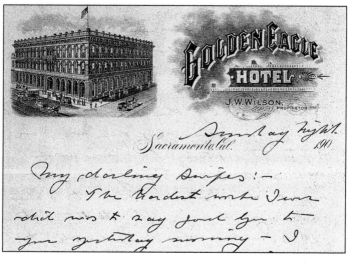

The next day, after passing through Stockton, they bought five gallons of gasoline in the town of Galt from a storekeeper who seemed bemused to see tourists in a horseless carriage. "The old man said when he got rich he was going to buy one of these – d – machines, so that he could spend his money fast," Jackson wrote Bertha. "He would break down his neighbor's fences . . . then he wouldn't have any money left for his children to fight over."

They stopped in Sacramento to make minor repairs to the *Vermont*— fixing the spark igniter, buying some second-hand tire tubes since no new ones were available, and attaching an acetylene headlamp to the front of the car for night driving because they already realized that the Winton's side lanterns were, Jackson said, "useless to illuminate the road."

During his stay in Sacramento, a delegation of local bicyclists, then a doctor, then a banker all offered Jackson advice on the roads ahead and gave him some rudimentary maps to pore over. He needed all the help he could get: a forbidding prospect lay before him. At the time, of the 2.3 million miles of road in the United States, fewer than 150 miles were paved, all of them within city limits. A mere 6 percent of the remaining road miles were considered "improved" (treated with gravel)—and virtually all of *those* were in the East. The rest were mostly dirt paths, suitable at best for horses, cows, and slow-moving wagons.

◄ *A place to buy gasoline*

Route 535—Keene, N. H., to Rutland, Vt.—73.3 m.

Reverse Route 634

Via Walpole, Bellows Falls, Chester, Ludlow, East Wallingford and East Clarendon.
Nearly all gravel; a few short stretches of dirt and macadam.

An important connection from southern New Hampshire, connecting at Rutland
with routes for the Lake Champlain district.

MILEAGE
Total Intermed.   For this and other exits see City Map, page 734.

0.0   0.0   **KEENE**, West & Main Sts., monument on right. Go west on
            West St. with trolley.

1.0   1.0   Right-hand diagonal street; bear right with trolley onto
            Park St.
                Left at 1.4 is Route 531 to Bennington.

2.6   1.6   3-corners; turn left with travel.

2.8   0.2   3-corners; bear right with travel.

3.4   0.6   Fork; bear left upgrade. Under RR. 4.9. Thru E. Westmore-
            land 7.5.

9.8   6.4   Fork; bear right with travel across small concrete bridge.

11.2 1.4   **Westmoreland**, 4-corners. Keep ahead.

11.7 0.5   Fork; bear left with travel. Avoid left-hand diagonal road
            12.1. Curve right and left across RR. 13.4.

14.8 3.1   Left-hand diagonal road; bear left across iron bridge.

16.9 2.1   End of road; bear left.

17.2 0.3   **Walpole, N. H.**, left-hand road at water-trough.
                HOTELS—Walpole Inn.
                    Straight ahead is Route 435 to Newport.
            Turn left. Cross RR. 17.7. Cross bridge over Connecticut
            River 17.8.

18.0 0.8   Go under RR. and at fork just beyond; bear right.
                Left fork is Route 586 to Greenfield.
                Bellows Falls City Map and Points of Interest, page 611.
            Cross long iron bridge 21.1, coming onto Westminster St.

21.5 3.5   Fork, fountain in center; bear right, curving right just
            beyond.

21.7 0.2   Fork; bear right, still on Westminster St.

21.9 0.2   **Bellows Falls, Vt.**, Westminster & Bridge Sts.; iron water-
            trough on right.
                HOTELS—Hotel Windham.
                GARAGES—Gates Garage, Westminster St.
            Keep ahead (north) on Westminster St., now with trolley.

22.2 0.3   End of street; bear left with trolley onto Rockingham St.

22.4 0.2   Fork, green in center, trolley turns left; bear right and turn
            right at end of street just beyond onto Atkinson St.

27.7 5.3   Fork; bear right with travel.

31.0 3.3   Left-hand road, school on right; turn left, keeping right 31.3.

34.7 3.7   Right-hand road; turn right.

34.8 0.1   Fork just beyond iron bridge; bear left, coming onto Main St.
                Right fork is Route 614 to Claremont.

| DAVIS GARAGE | 4 DOORS BELOW HOTEL FULLERTON |
| CHESTER   VERMONT | Storage—Accessories—Expert Mechanics
Battery Charging |

| **THE FULLERTON**
CHESTER, VT.
MEALS AT ALL HOURS
Telephone 8020 | Chicken Dinner noon and night, $1.00   GARAGE
Rates, $3.00 to $5.00 per day   Our own garden.
Run in connection with Rowell's Inn at Simonsville
JOHN A. ROWELL, Prop.
Mt. Holyoke Hotel, Northampton, Mass., under same management |

TO CHICAGO

TO HOTEL

Some early guidebooks included photographs to identify important forks in the road.

Roads were not only bad, for the most part they were also unmarked, since the only people who usually traveled them were local residents who didn't need signs to tell them which turn to take. By 1903 a few companies had begun publishing guidebooks with detailed instructions on how to get from one town to the next— compilations of lists (such as, "Start at Civil War monument. Go west 1.3 miles to granite watering trough. Turn left for 0.6 miles. Bear right under railroad overpass. Go 0.4 miles to white house." Etc., etc.) that might go on for two pages simply to cover a twenty-mile trip. But these books, cumbersome as they might be, were available only for heavily populated portions of the East. In the West, where the roads were much worse and the distances much vaster, no one had yet bothered to publish guidebooks.

A new headlamp for the **Vermont**

To cross the continent, Jackson decided it would be best to follow the routes of railroads as much as possible— to use their rights-of-way as a road if necessary, even use their trestles in places where no other bridge could be found. And to avoid the sandy wastes of Nevada, which had defeated Alexander Winton two years earlier, he determined to detour north, through Oregon, even though it would add more than a thousand miles to his journey and for a while take him through places where even railroads did not exist. Despite all the obstacles in his path, Jackson optimistically planned on averaging up to two hundred miles a day across the continent.

My darling Swipes—

We leave in the morning for Oroville . . . the last railway point we will have until we strike Ontario, [Oregon]. When we get there the worst will be over.

I can run the car as well as Crocker & have rather surprised him. . . . We take 2 hours on and 2 off at the wheel. . . . He is a mighty good man.

. . . I am fine . . . & the only trouble is I miss you so.

Nelson

Please keep my letters as I want them for reference.

On May 25, they started for Oroville, traveling through miles and miles of fruit orchards on dusty roads Jackson described as "a compound of ruts, bumps, and thank-you-marms." "We never noticed," he added, "as our cooking utensils jolted off one by one. When we discovered our loss, we could not afford to turn back to seek them."

Then they discovered something else: they were lost. Their fortunes seemed to brighten, Jackson later remembered, when they came upon a red-haired young woman riding a white horse:

"Which way to Marysville?" I asked her.

"Right down that road," she said and pointed. We took that road for about 50 miles and then it came to a dead end at an isolated farmhouse. The family all turned out to stare at us and told us we'd have to go back.

We went back, and met the red-haired young woman again.

"Why did you send us way down there?" I asked her.

"I wanted paw and maw and my husband to see you," she said. "They've never seen an automobile."

Long after nightfall, they finally pulled into Oroville by the light of their new searchlight. "Everything is all O.K.," a tired Jackson wrote his wife. "I shall take my car through to New York," he promised, underlining the words for emphasis before signing the letter, "yours till death."

He awoke the next morning planning to reach the town of Alturas, 158 miles to the northeast, before nightfall. But shortly after setting off, he learned that snows on the mountain passes blocked the direct route he had hoped to take through the northern Sierra Nevada. So they detoured *northwest* through the valley towns of Chico, Nord, Vina, Tehama, and Redbluff, over steadily deteriorating roads (with the brief exception of a few miles near Vina, where the late railroad magnate Leland Stanford had invested in improvements near one of his

Next stop . . . the mountains! ➤

Climbing a rocky trail

Cooling the tires in a stream

estates). "Ahead of us, like a guidepost, towered Mount Shasta," Jackson wrote. But with each mile it was leading them away from, not closer to, their ultimate destination.

After covering 114 miles, they chugged into the tiny hamlet of Anderson, where they put the *Vermont* in a livery stable and checked into the town's only hotel, hoping for a good night's sleep to prepare for crossing the lower mountain passes of the Cascades. But bedbugs drove them out of their room, and they spent the remainder of the night trying to sleep in their car.

Early on the morning of May 27, the ascent into the mountains began. They climbed steep, rocky trails no automobile had ever traveled—"mostly low-gear work," Jackson wrote, that required frequent stops for Crocker to fix the clutch. The spark igniter faltered again and they stopped to get it working correctly. Yet more stops occurred when sharp stones pierced the car's tires; they patched the inner tubes and reinflated them by hand pump, then pushed on.

Often the trail narrowed to ten feet—one-way thoroughfares established by nature. Sometimes it was necessary to remove boulder blockades by hand.

Slipping on shale and loose rocks, weaving around mountain ledges, we staked our careers against none-too-reliable brakes on steep descents . . . [around] hairpin turns where, jolting and skidding, we suddenly looked down unfenced sheer precipices.

The winding trail was crisscrossed by mountain streams, usually with no bridges over them. Jackson and Crocker had no choice but to put the *Vermont* into high gear and try to get across at top speed. "We welcomed" some of the creeks, Jackson said, "to let the car's hot tires cool." But one creek was too deep, and the *Vermont* got stuck in midstream. The men took off their shoes and pants, waded to the other shore with the block and tackle, attached it to a tree, pulled the car out with the rope, and then continued on the bumpy road. "We were lucky not to have lost our block and tackle, for bit by bit our equipment was disappearing, including my own spectacles and fountain pen," Jackson wrote.

They passed through Bella Vista and Round Mountain, were forced to pay a four-dollar toll to use a privately owned stretch of "bad, rocky, mountain road" and, after covering sixty-nine miles in twelve hard hours, finally made it to Montgomery for the night. Their troubles worsened the next day:

36 *Took 5 gal of gasoline & left Montgomery at 8:45 hoping to get to Fall River for lunch but got off the wrong road & lost 20 miles. Found bridge down & lost 14 more.*

Tire blew up twice & repaired it with rope—are now running on rope.

At Burney we had . . . our clutch fixed & gave him "two bits". Reached Fall River at 4:30. Took ten gal of gasoline—still climbing, snow all around us. Roads very narrow & rocky.

On the road we ran out of cylinder oil & we had a storage tank in the inside of the boot with a tap running down through the bottom of the carriage. The tap got stuck, so Crocker crawled under the carriage with a wrench. He was lying on his back, he started the tap, but couldn't stop it & got 2 gal of oil in the chest & face. He is now wearing my clothes & the others are on the side of the road.

During it all, Jackson somehow lost yet another pair of spectacles while the *Vermont* bounced along. But he couldn't help admiring the scenery—dramatic vistas of mountain peaks and the ancient volcanic cone of Lassen Peak at one turn; at another, a vertiginous view down a narrow canyon to a beautiful waterfall on the

Crocker cleans up

Through the forest

Pit River a thousand feet below their trail. "A grand sight," he wrote to Bertha. "I never went through such country in my life."

Mount Shasta now faded completely from sight behind them as they wound through dense stands of Ponderosa pines, and finally came down out of the Cascades and headed for Alturas, in the northeastern corner of California—seven hundred miles, by Jackson's calculations, from their starting point. The one-day trip he had so blithely planned from Oroville had turned into four days of breakdowns, repairs, and delays.

> *Alturas, "Nowhere"*
> *3 miles back of sundown*
> *Saturday morning*
> *My darling Girl:—*
>
> *We have crossed the mountains & don't expect to come to anymore until we get into Idaho. . . . We have proven that my machine can do or go anywhere.*
>
> *. . . How I wish you were with me, & that it was possible for you to take the trip—I feel confident we can make it.*
>
> *With . . . a barrell full [of love], I am, as always, yours.*
>
> *Nelson*

CHAPTER THREE

ONE OF THE WONDERS OF THE CENTURY

Quite a flurry of excitement was erected [Friday] evening by the arrival of an automobile. Very few of our citizens had ever seen this, one of the wonders of the century, and large crowds gazed with curious interest at the horseless wagon. The Indians especially never tired of gazing at the machine. Indeed had a flying machine lit down in their midst it would not have created greater astonishment.

—Alturas Plain Dealer

In the town of Alturas, Jackson decided to wait for a day. On his way through the mountains he had telegraphed back to San Francisco for a new set of badly needed tires, some new batteries, and a new cyclometer to help him measure distances—and he had been promised by Wells, Fargo that a stagecoach with his shipment would soon catch up with him.

One day passed. Then a second and a third. Still no tires.

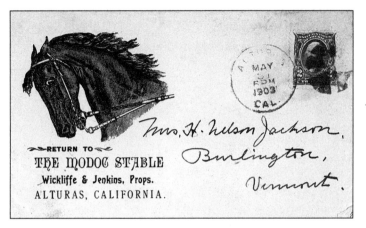

Monday, June 1st.
Well Old Girl,

I am rather provoked over our delay. . . . I have lost 5½ days. This is a bad start for our first eleven days out. Just as soon as I can get decent tires we will make a record run. I feel more confident that I can make New York. Crocker is more interested than ever & is keeping the machine up in good shape.

. . . It is hotter than blazes today & I wish we were on the road. We are causing a great sensation along

the road—it is the first machine that has ever gone over these mountains. Yesterday the farmers drove in for miles to see my machine & there has been a hundred people around the livery stable since our arrival. I have been offered all prices to take them for a ride. I have promised some of the cow punchers a ride if they will get me up a good round up. They are planning it for this afternoon & I expect to see a regular Wild West show.*

Reveling in the avalanche of attention he and his machine were attracting (the Alturas *New Era* had proclaimed: "Quite a Sight for Alturasites: A Real Live Auto Steams into Town"), Jackson nonetheless had become frustrated by the long wait for new tires. More than half his time on the road so far had been consumed by such delays. "I don't believe we would appreciate our trip if we didn't have these accidents &c," Jackson wrote his wife, but "if it hadn't been for our tires we would have

◄ Bystanders in Alturas, California

been in Ontario today." Obviously concerned that Bertha might be getting equally impatient for him to make better progress, Jackson assured her, "I know that you know what this trip will mean to me if I can carry it through & that *I will*. So you will be brave & patient until I come—I know it is hard but it is also for me—I miss you so. I shall rush it through."

By Tuesday, June 2, when the shipment still had not arrived, Jackson decided to leave Alturas anyway—"in no very good humor," according to the local paper. Still, a large crowd gathered to see him and Crocker off with many handshakes. The *Plain Dealer* expressed their sentiment: "We join with all of our citizens in wishing the Doctor and his companion a God-speed and a happy termination of his journey."

With its rear tires wrapped in rawhide and rope, the *Vermont* pulled out of Alturas. Despite the tires' condition,

Pulling into Lakeview, Oregon

Jackson expected to make good time now that he was out of the mountains, and he had set his sights for the day on Burns, Oregon, 220 miles to the northeast. But only a few miles into the morning, a front spring broke, and the *Vermont* limped along at under ten miles per hour. (Even at that pace, Jackson's sun cap, coat, and another fountain pen somehow jostled loose and fell by the wayside.)

Six hours later, they reached Lakeview, Oregon, where it seemed as if the whole town was waiting for them. The crowd had been building since early morning, after being alerted by telegram that the "wonder," as the *Lakeview Herald* called it, was on its way, and since the *Vermont* would be the first automobile ever to reach Lake County, "this was enough to put every man, woman and child in Lakeview on the keen edge of expectancy." The competing paper, the *Lake County Examiner,* was even more breathless:

First Automobile in Lake County.

The first automobile to visit Lake county arrived in Lakeview Tuesday afternoon, about 4 o'clock, having spent six hours on the road from Alturas to this place, a distance of 60 miles. The wonderful machine would have made much better time had it not been for the the accidental breaking of one of the main springs over the front

FIRST AUTO.
SEEN IN C. VIS

The way the streets of Lakeview were lined with people Tuesday afternoon, one would think a circus was coming to town, or a 4th of July procession was about to pass. While it was neither, the people's curiosity had been aroused from a report that an automobile was coming this way, and that if they wished to see it pass it was necessary to have a seat in the front row, otherwise it might go through at the rate of 90 miles an hour, and would be out of sight before they could run a block.

It hove in sight at just 4 o'clock and the crowds surged forward to get a first look at a real live auto, a machine that nine-tenths of the people of Lake County had never seen. The machine drove up in front of the Hotel Lakeview and stopped. The Chauffeur enquired for a blacksmith shop, having had a mishap coming over the rough roads.

A local blacksmith was put to work fixing the front spring, never sensing, Jackson said, "that our strange vehicle was a symbol of doom to [his] profession." And a local merchant charged him three dollars a gallon for gasoline, nearly ten times the average price in most cities. The next day, Jackson wanted to get moving again, even though the repairs weren't completed until midafternoon.

Mr. Lake's bicycle shop

◁ *A Lakeview citizen poses behind the wheel.*

Just as we were ready and had left the blacksmith shop the inner tube gave way and we ran to the outskirts of the village to repair it. We went over what inner tubes we had and found that they were rotten. We put three patches on the best one and succeeded into getting air into it at about 5 o'clock and away we started; but old Cat Fate was against us, for we only ran 3 miles then she blew again.

They had no choice now but to return to Lakeview and wait for the stagecoach to reach them with the supplies they had ordered from San Francisco.

Thursday. Loafed all day and kept [the telegraph] wire busy to keep in touch with the tires. They left Madelaine tonight. We spent most of the day in Mr. Lake's bicycle shop and Crocker made $3.00 repairing a Columbian bicycle. . . .

Some of the people here have never seen a railroad or been away from the place for more than fifty miles. A little boy asked his teacher if he could have a holiday to see the auto.

Friday. I have just received word that my tires left Alturas early this morning, so they will be here tonight. Spent day killing time.

New tires, but a rough road

Late on the night of June 5, the stagecoach with the tires, batteries, and cyclometer finally arrived—and by early the next morning, Jackson and Crocker had everything ready. Ahead of them lay nearly three hundred miles of Oregon desert, a barely inhabited area that had the added distinction of being farther from a railroad than any other place in the United States. Jackson hoped to cross it in two days and reach Ontario, where he had telegraphed ahead for more tires and supplies to be waiting for him at the train station.

At six a.m., they set off from Lakeview for their dash across the desert, but almost immediately got confused and went nineteen miles down the wrong road before realizing it. By eight o'clock thick dust was already clogging one of the *Vermont's* two carburetors and they had to stop to clean it. Then the car wouldn't start; the new batteries were defective. Time after time, they struggled to get a sufficient spark, but with no luck. Hours ticked by. Crocker tried everything he could think of to coax the *Vermont* to life, but still it refused. Noontime came and went; then most of the afternoon.

About four o'clock they spotted a cowpuncher in the distance and Jackson called him to them by firing his gun. A few minutes later, the 20-horsepower automobile

A one-horsepower towing service

that people had called "one of the wonders of the century" found itself lassoed and being dragged like a stubborn calf across the desert floor by a cowboy and his horse.

The cowboy towed them to the nearest ranch house, where Crocker again went to work and at last got the *Vermont* running. They set off immediately, following what Jackson called "the damn[ed]est, rough, rocky, sandy road this side of Haydes." The route also took them along the shore of Lake Abert, whose alkali-impregnated waters put off a pungent smell. "Fortunately for us," Jackson wrote his wife, "our aulfactory [*sic*] centers are not very sensitive." Fourteen long hours after leaving Lakeview, they reached a ranch called the SL.

The ranchman kindly offered to give us his attic for the night, so we crawled up the ladder for bed. Here we found a pile of rags in one corner with two blankets that every settler coming that way since forty-nine had slept under. It is needless to say that we each sat on a nail keg and waited for our host and hostess to get to sleep. This we soon discovered from the sonorous sound that came up through the planks of our floor, whereupon we both jumped out of the window and

Arrival at the ranch

had a very comfortable night in one of the horse stalls in the barn.

Somehow, word of their troubles filtered back to the *Lake County Examiner.* "If they meet with as many accidents and are delayed as long as they were in Alturas and Lakeview," the newspaper reported, "it will be winter before they see the Atlantic."

On the morning of June 7, Jackson and Crocker resumed their journey across the desert—and soon encountered homesteaders traveling by wagon to some of the only free land still available in the nation.

> *I cannot see why they come to this desert, but the Oregon agents seem to be able to paint them a most beautiful picture of the homesteads here. One poor fellow, seeing us coming down the road, thought the train had got off the track, so hastily unharnessed his horses and he and his wife crawled under the wagon.*
>
> *Of course when we came along we frightened their horses and they ran many miles across the desert. I was very sorry for the poor fellow but he was green as they make them.*

They passed the dry bed of Alkali Lake and the almost invisible hamlet of Wagontire, where the roads became so rough Jackson and Crocker decided instead to make their way through the endless sagebrush, which soon stripped off their new cyclometer, making it impossible to measure distances. And somewhere along the way, the gasoline in their storage tank leaked out. When they reached an outpost called Oakerman's on Silver Creek that evening, they had less than a quart left.

It was twenty-six miles to Burns, the nearest town where gas might be available. With no telephone at Oakerman's, Jackson rented the owner's bicycle and sent Crocker off on it. He was gone all night and half the next day—forced to *walk* most of the distance when his bicycle tire was punctured—and finally returned with four gallons of gasoline and three gallons of benzine which, Jackson complained, cost him nearly twenty dollars.

But the supply of fuel got them to Burns, where a local doctor gave them five gallons of gasoline, and then to Harney, where they purchased fifteen gallons more. Farther east, a ranch wife fed them a good meal but didn't have any extra beds or even a stable to offer them, so they slept on the ground next to the *Vermont*—a fitful night, Jackson

A homesteader's horses, about to have their meal interrupted

reported, constantly interrupted by a sow and her noisy piglets.

They began their fourth day in the desert with more than a hundred miles yet to go. But the car kept grinding to a halt every time the undercarriage got hung up on the high crown in the center of the rutted road, sometimes requiring the men to use jacks to set it free. They bought lunch at a ranch that Jackson called "the dirtiest place I ever saw," and then, in the afternoon, the front spring broke yet again, delaying them once more. The only comfort was a hot spring they encountered, where, Jackson wrote, "we had a mighty good, *necessary* wash."

Pressing on in the evening, they discovered to their dismay that they had run out of cylinder oil. This time it was Jackson's turn to walk for help.

It was very dark indeed and I did not like at all the idea of trying to find someone, not knowing where they lived or how far I will have to go to find them. After walking about an hour there was an awful commotion in front of me which made my hair stand on ends and my legs run about a hundred yards as fast as they could go. It was nothing but a poor cow that I had disturbed on its night slumbers. I haven't got over it yet.

By whistling I managed to raise a dog and by following the sound of its bark found an old ranchman and when I told him where we were he said if we had gone over the first hill for about half a mile we would have got into Vale. I got back about half past three. Then we proceeded to Vale, making that night and day 112 miles.

In Vale, they finally found some cylinder oil, and late on the afternoon of June 10, their nineteenth day on the road, they motored the last seventeen miles to Ontario, Oregon, a town near the Idaho border and, more important, a stop on the Oregon Shortline Railroad. Waiting for them at the station were a full set of new tires and a new front spring.

"When we saw the railroad," Jackson told his wife, "we both felt like throwing up our hats and giving three cheers."

◁ *The citizens of Burns, Oregon, turn out to inspect the* **Vermont.**

CHAPTER FOUR

AN ENTHUSIAST FOR MOTORING

Thursday, June 11.
My dear Swipes,
We put on our new springs and one
new tire and left Ontario a little after
four. . . . We crossed the Snake River
by a ferry [and] are now in Idaho. . . .

Shortly after we left, it com-
menced to rain and for the first time
we had to take out our rubber
clothing. This made travelling very
bad. . . . We found a stream to ford
and thought of course we could make
it as we had many others, by shooting
it. But the mud was very deep and
we got stuck in the center of it. So for
the second time we had to use our
block and tackle. . . .

The rain was coming down in buckets and we had to work a good deal up to our knees in mud and did not arrive in Caldwell until twelve o'clock at night and then soaking wet.

We put up at the Pacific Hotel and the people noticed we were carrying with us a very strong odor. . . . We had run over a gernarium pussy [skunk].

As early in the trip as Sacramento (and for reasons unexplained), Jackson had been looking for a small dog to accompany him on his attempt to cross the continent. In Idaho, he finally got his chance —thanks to the kind of misadventure that had now become almost routine. They had pulled out of Caldwell early on the morning of June 12, but after driving a few miles Jackson realized he had left his coat at the hotel. "On our way back," he wrote Bertha, "we were stopped by a man and asked if I didn't want a dog for a mascot. As I had been trying to steal one we were glad to get him so accepted the present (consideration $15.00). So Bud is now with us."

Bud: ready for the road

Bud was a young, light-colored bull-dog, and whatever the rationale for adding this third member to the expedition, he almost immediately began attracting as much attention as the *Vermont*. (Crossing the continent a century earlier, Meriwether Lewis had brought along a Newfoundland dog named Seaman—for which he paid twenty dollars—and it, too, created considerable stir among the natives they encountered.) Some newspapers would report that Jackson had rescued Bud from a savage dog fight; others wrote that he was a lonesome stray who had chased after the car for two miles before being taken on board.

"Bud soon became an enthusiast for motoring," Jackson bragged, especially after his masters put a pair of their goggles on him to keep the stinging, alkali dust out of his eyes. Riding in front, Bud learned to watch the road ahead as intently as Crocker and Jackson, bracing himself for every bump and turn—and becoming, his owner said, "the one member of [our] trio who used no profanity on the entire trip."

◄ Main Street in Hailey, Idaho

➤ ➤ ➤ ➤ ➤ ➤ ➤ ➤ *June 11, to Caldwell, Idaho* ➤ ➤

57

A driver's nightmare

Raingear for an entire car

The day of Bud's arrival ended as it had begun. Even though he was now taking roads that paralleled the railroad tracks and planned on making up for lost time, Jackson got bad advice in Nampa and followed the wrong set of tracks, which took them thirty-eight miles out of their way before they realized it and had to backtrack. At the end of fifteen hours on the road, they reached the town of Orchard at eleven p.m., a mere forty-five miles from their starting point. The three of them spent their first night together sleeping under the car.

When they arrived in Mountain Home the next day, the local newspaper reported that the *Vermont,* "being the first horseless carriage in the village . . . created quite a sensation and attracted crowds of curious [people] who surrounded it as flies surround a keg of sorghum."

The rains that greeted them to Idaho had not let up, and hearing reports that the main road to Pocatello would be difficult, Jackson impulsively detoured northeast again, this time toward the town of Hailey at the edge of the Sawtooth Mountains, thinking conditions might improve. They didn't.

The roads were extremely bad and wet and many times we had great difficulty in pulling the car out of the mud. We got stuck good and fast about seven in

A 1902 Oldsmobile slogs ahead

the evening and after working two hours with our block and tackle we finally had to give it up. We made a little tent out of our mackintoshes and crawled into our sleeping bags for the night.

Adding to their misery, Bud had become sick after drinking some alkali water. (In his letter to Bertha, Jackson spared her the details on the symptoms.) The next morning, one of them hiked half a mile to a sheepherder's cabin and persuaded him to bring his horses to pull them out. For the rest of the trip, in honor of the combined effort of the *Vermont's* engine and the team of horses, Jackson would refer to the place as the "twenty-four horsepower stream." And as he had several times already on the trip, Jackson paid for the services (and a home-cooked meal) by providing his host with a short ride on what some locals were now calling the "Go-Like-Hell Machine."

In Hailey, Jackson telegraphed the Winton Company in Cleveland, placing an order for them to ship him a new air intake pipe, since the original had dropped off somewhere along the road. It was the first time he had contacted the company directly—and the first time Winton officials became aware that one of their cars was trying to cross the continent.

Their detour next took them through what is now Craters of the Moon National Monument, a desolate, eerie landscape shaped and reshaped by a series of volcanic cataclysms. "The country took on a new character," Jackson wrote, "soaring heights of denuded slopes, monstrous cliffs, and giant boulders scattered in magnificent confusion." Sixty years *before* Jackson, wagon trains of pioneers had ventured this way on what was called the "Goodale's Cutoff" on the Oregon Trail. Sixty years *after* Jackson, astronauts would be brought there to train for the first lunar landing.

Traveling south now, along the edges of the vast Snake River lava beds, they reached the towns of Blackfoot and Pocatello, then took what Jackson called "an exceptionally good road" that followed the rail line and allowed them to open the *Vermont's* throttle as they whirled into the quiet village of Soda Springs, where the local paper, *The Idanha Chieftain*, announced his arrival under the headline: "It Startled the Natives."

The first automobile to invade Soda Springs rounded the corner at Whitman's store just at sundown Tuesday night, and with a toot that sounded like a young fog horn, whizzed up Dillon Street and stopped at the Idanha Hotel.

*When the cowboys,
sheep herders and
Indians recovered from
their surprise they
caught their breath and
let out a whoop that
was taken up and
passed along the entire
length of the block. The
interest in "roulette"
and "twenty-one" was
temporarily suspended
until the strange
machine had been
thoroughly examined
and the curiosity of the
crowd appeased.*

In Soda Springs, Jackson discovered that yet
another personal item had
fallen off the bouncing
car. This time it was another coat, with most of his remaining cash. He telegraphed Bertha to wire him two hundred
dollars, in care of the Western Union office in Cheyenne,

Soda Springs, Idaho

Wyoming, a city more than 350 miles to the east, which
Jackson (despite all his experiences on the trip to the contrary) felt confident he could reach in a few days.

64   On June 17, they rattled off toward Wyoming and quickly made thirty miles—until the hub and bearings on a front wheel gave out. In Montpelier, Idaho, they borrowed some bearings from a farmer's mowing machine and had a local blacksmith install them with a cone he crafted out of iron. The delay cost them the rest of the day, but Jackson's optimism was undiminished.

> *Hotel Burgoyne, Montpelier, Idaho. Wednesday*
> *Darling Swipes—*
>   *Just a line to say that everything is alright with*
> *your wandering boy. I can't write much, as we sleep,*
> *then work. We arrived here at 12 o'clock this noon*
> *with the running gear of one of the front wheels gone.*
> *We have it patched up & shall leave in the morning*
> *hoping that it will take us to Cheyenne.*
>   *When you hear that we have reached Rawlins,*
> *Wyoming, you will know that I can make the trip a*
> *go—so bet all the money you have got on it.*
>   *. . . Well old girlie, I can't say any more—you know*
> *how I feel. I shall make up for lost time.*

Soon after crossing into Wyoming the next day, the blacksmith's iron cone fell apart. They inched their way to Diamondville, site of a large coal mine, where a machinist

Coal mine in Diamondville, Wyoming ➤

offered to help Crocker make a new cone out of tempered steel. They slept that night in the machine shop, made the repairs the next morning, "and after giving all hands a ride," Jackson wrote, got a late-afternoon start for the town of Opal: "Just as it was getting dark we [got] stuck in a deep mud hole and I walked thirteen miles to get someone to pull us out. I got back about 3 o'clock and we worked from that time until nine in the morning drying up our wet batteries."

Things got even worse on June 20. A tremendous cloudburst struck the area after they passed through the town of Granger, flooding and washing out the road they were following. They resorted to trying to navigate across the badlands—cutting bundles of the ubiquitous sagebrush

. . . and repairs in the open sage

to place under the spinning tires in muddy spots, getting out the block and tackle when the car got stuck, changing direction every time they encountered a gully too deep to cross, and getting hopelessly lost. "We zigzagged as best we could," Jackson wrote. "Sometimes we went north instead of east; at others we even went north*west* . . . bringing us back . . . where we had been before." They struggled along for hours, ultimately going, by Jackson's estimates, sixty-nine miles out of their way.

> *Coming to the bank of a river, we judged from our maps and compass that it was [the] Green River, and we resolved to follow its downward course. . . . When night came on we made camp beside the car, and . . . having lost our cooking outfit and provisions, and being in an uninhabited region . . . went to bed without any supper.*

Their roadless meanderings had brought them to a place that had challenged countless other overlanders in American history. Not far to the east was the famous "Parting of the Ways," where pioneers who had just crossed the Continental Divide at South Pass faced the first of many agonizing choices between which trail to take—cutoffs promising a more direct route but a potentially fatal lack of water versus a longer trail whose oxbow curves kept closer to streams and rivers but might mean slower progress and the chance of being caught in mountains farther west when winter set in. Forty-niners on their way to California had passed this way. So had the Mormons. So had the doomed Donner Party.

Jackson and Crocker had now been on the road for twenty-nine days. Of them all, this day had already proved to be the most disconcerting and potentially discouraging— the violent storm, the washed-out roads, and the confusing maze of gullies that had finally deposited them, wet and hungry, on the banks of a river too big to cross. But as they went to sleep that night, they were luckily unaware of something that would only have added to their worries.

Back in San Francisco, two other men had departed on their own car trip across the continent.

———————

San Francisco, June 20th, 1903.
At 2 o'clock, [Tom] Fetch . . . mounted and took his place at the steering wheel. Beside him, [I] took [my] seat, and now, without further formalities, the course was steered to the famous Cliff House in San Francisco, overlooking the Pacific Ocean and the Seal Rocks, thence to depart with a few whiffs of salt breeze to cheer our memory on the long land-bound expedition.

—Marius Krarup

PACKARD

The Car Ahead

WITH A HALF TURN OF THE STARTING CRANK
and one filling of supplies the owner of a **PACKARD** car is
ready for one mile or two hundred and seventy-five. In a go-as-
you-please, cross-country tour he asks odds of no man, but by the
irresistible, almost brutal regularity with which he leaves the miles
behind he is able to get there every time on time and to get back. In
this big country of ours, with its average indifferent roads, even abnormal
power and excessive gearing are alike unable to cope with the combination
of perfect parts in the **PACKARD**. It is the most reliable motor car ever built.

"Ask the Man Who Owns One"

Printed matter pertaining to any of these perform-
ances mailed upon application to Department P.

Seats 5 People   Price $2,500

"LICENSED MANUFACTURERS UNDER SELDEN PATENTS"
PACKARD MOTOR CAR COMPANY, Warren, Ohio

Tom Fetch and Marius Krarup had been chosen by the
Packard Motor Company to drive one of its brand-new
12-horsepower touring cars from San Francisco to New
York. Fetch was a test driver for the company; Krarup was
a reporter for *Automobile* magazine, going along to file
regular reports on what Packard's advertising chief admitted was "a spectacle" to attract public attention and prove
the car's durability. For three months—well before Jackson
had ever made his rash bet—the Packard Company had
been planning their trip.

It was everything that Jackson's expedition was not. The
Packard had been modified to carry more gasoline and
have better gearing for steep mountain grades. Each day's
itinerary along the main route of the transcontinental railroad had been predetermined, with extra supplies already
placed at strategic points, and the men's personal luggage
shipped ahead by train each morning to the next stopping
place. To help with any mechanical problems, an expert
machinist from the Packard factory in Warren, Ohio, was
even sent along—riding in the car some days, taking the
train ahead on others.

Pulling out of San Francisco on June 20, Fetch and
Krarup made excellent time right from the start. By the
fifth day, they had crossed the summits of the Sierra
Nevada at Lake Tahoe and descended into Carson City,

Overleaf: *The railroad keeps Fetch and Krarup well-supplied.* ➤

Nevada. Learning from Alexander Winton's disaster with deep sand two years earlier, they came equipped with two long strips of heavy canvas to roll out across soft spots and provide enough traction to keep from bogging down.

On their first day on the Nevada desert they covered more than seventy miles—and felt confident enough about their progress to take the next day off in Wadsworth, simply to wait for more film for Krarup's camera. When they left, they carried with them a case of twelve bottles of beer packed in ice. Krarup wrote:

> *In the immediate vicinity of the town rises a sandhill of formidable proportions. . . . Such is the tradition of its terrors that the town cheerfully expected us to*

Fetch and Krarup roll through Nevada.

return for reinforcements . . . and when we arrived at the top we found an enterprising man awaiting developments with a team, rope and tackle in readiness for our expected emergency, as well as a crowd of interested spectators. Broad minded enough to see that the laugh was on them, they cheered us loudly as we passed.

As they cruised across the desert in a direct line toward New York, everyone they met was impressed with their meticulous preparation and astonished at their progress. And everywhere they went, Fetch and Krarup steadfastly ignored the fact that Jackson was already on the road. A mere ten days out from San Francisco, they were already halfway across Nevada.

Canvas strips help conquer the soft sands. ➤

CHAPTER FIVE

THE WORST OF IT IS OVER

Jackson awoke along the banks of the Green River on the morning of June 21, still lost in western Wyoming, after suffering through a night he described as the time that "thirty thousand mosquitoes died on the back of my neck."

But his more immediate concern was food. It had been nearly thirty-six hours since he and Crocker had last eaten— and both of them, he joked later, "were stealing speculative glances at Bud as we tightened our belts."

They followed the river south—hoping it would lead them to a town or a homestead. Instead, they finally came upon a lonely sheepherder, who said he hadn't seen another human being in three weeks and happily offered them a feast of roast lamb and boiled corn—"the finest meal," Jackson said, "I ever ate." When the sheepherder refused to be paid for the food, Jackson insisted that he at least accept a rifle as a token of appreciation. "If he had asked us then for my car," Jackson added, "I believe we would have given it to him."

With full bellies and the directions the sheepherder provided them, Jackson and Crocker were soon heading east once more, along the route that would one day become the famed Lincoln Highway, and half a century after that, Interstate 80, the principal thoroughfare across the nation. It paralleled the transcontinental railroad line and took them through the towns of Bryan, Green River, and Rock Springs. A circus arrived by rail in Rock Springs the same day, Jackson wrote his wife, "and we are taken for part of the show."

Timely help from three Italians

My Dear Swipes—

They are charging me 60 cents a gallon [for gasoline] and as there is no pay station between here and Cheyenne I am unable to get any money from there.

The roads are still watched frightfully and we are spending most of the time trying to get out of water and mud holes. We buried our car completely in one and after working a half day to get it out again, three Italians came along, each packing a heavy bag. I explained to them that the next stop was twelve miles away and that if they would help us out I would take their baggage in for them. This they consented to do and in about an hour we were on our way again.

After delivering their luggage to the section boss we started on for Bitter Creek, crossing two rivers over the railroad bridge. . . . We had no trouble in crossing railroad bridges. With practice, bumping over bridge ties is no great task. Sometimes, though, we had to hunt for five miles to find

◄ *A sheepherder greets Crocker and the* **Vermont.**

➤　　➤　　➤　　➤　　*June 22, stuck west of Bitter Creek, Wyoming*　　➤

Two hands versus twenty horsepower

a place where we could get our machine on the rail-road track.

. . . About eight o'clock we struck another deep mud hole so camped beside it for the night. In the morning we spent about two hours filling it up with sage brush and in shooting it we broke the upper leaf of our rear spring. We then crawled into Bitter Creek.

At the train stop of Bitter Creek, Jackson found himself entirely out of cash and pawned his watch for ten dollars from the station agent. From the depot he telegraphed Bertha a brief—but descriptive—message: "Rain, washout, bum roads and luck, broken spring. Crawl to Rawlins."

They pressed on, encountering deep sand holes that required them to get out the block and tackle and hook it to an anchor they drove into more solid ground (there being no trees anywhere in sight). Then they would attach the rope to the car's rear axle, whose spinning would slowly winch them out once the engine was started.

In other places, they had to dig themselves out by hand. "I have done nothing but use my hands in place of my 20 horsepower engine to propel my car from Granger to here," Jackson wrote Bertha, "and the only thing that I can handle now with safety is my knife and fork."

June 23, to Rawlins, Wyoming

Downtown in Rawlins, Wyoming

in a livery stable down the street, the *Vermont* came to a noisy and sudden stop. The stud bolts holding the connecting rod to the crankshaft sheared off, and it pierced through the crankcase cover—the worst mechanical breakdown to date.

This was a problem that could not be fixed without new parts from the Winton factory in Ohio. Jackson had no choice but to telegraph the company and wait for a train to deliver them. "We could not possibly have much worse luck than we have during the past three days and we have had enough to discourage any army," Jackson wrote his wife, "but I will bring my car through to New York if it takes a leg."

On June 23, exactly one month after leaving San Francisco, they pulled into the town of Rawlins and made arrangements to stay at the Ferris Hotel, looking forward to their first comfortable bed in nearly a week. But as Jackson and Crocker drove the short distance to park their car

Driving into Rawlins, Jackson and Crocker became inadvertently drawn into a minor drama being played out in small towns all across America at the dawn of the auto era: the gamesmanship for bragging rights over who would be the town's first car owner. In Rawlins, the participants were Dr. John Osborne and Henry Murchison.

Osborne, an ex-governor and one of the town's most prominent citizens, had let it be known in late 1901 that the distinction would be his, as soon as his "Champion Favorite" arrived from the East. But then a fire at the factory disrupted production, and word circulated that Osborne's delivery had been postponed. Sensing an opportunity, Murchison quietly placed a rush order for an eight-passenger steam-powered machine called the "Red Devil" from a San Francisco company.

Rawlins's first automobile arrived by train on April 5, 1902. It was Murchison's—but it had been shipped in parts and apparently without all the instructions for assembly. With local assistance (and no doubt a lot of joking advice from a gallery of onlookers), he finally managed to put the car together. But despite his every effort, he could not get it started.

The Red Devil was still sitting in the street, immobile, when a freight train unloaded Osborne's Champion Favorite on April 23. Fully assembled, it was motoring around the streets of Rawlins within hours, Osborne sitting proudly at the wheel. Weeks passed, then months. As Osborne went to and from his office, made his house calls, took small pleasure jaunts in his new car, all the while basking in the town's attention and envy, Murchison could only watch from the seat of an auto that wouldn't move. The embarrassment eventually became so acute that he quietly pushed his vehicle into a storage shed and out of sight.

Then Jackson and Crocker drove into town—and for the first time in nearly a year and a half, hope stirred in Henry Murchison's heart. He brought Crocker to the shed where the listless Red Devil had been housed, explained his dilemma, and begged for help.

The next edition of the Rawlins *Republican* told the result. Under the headline, "Murchison's 'Mobile Is Alright," the newspaper announced that "yesterday Henry Murchison was seen driving around the city in his horse-less carriage, which he has been unable to use on account of not being able to generate power to keep it going." The brief story duly credited Crocker for the machine's transformation—and then hinted that Murchison's competitive fire had also been rekindled. "He is considering a trip to New York," the paper said, "and if he does he will overtake Dr. Nelson [*sic*] before he gets half way."

Dr. Osborne (dark suit) makes his rounds. ➤

82 For his part, Jackson spent the five days they were
stuck in Rawlins arranging for his bank to send him more
money, writing long letters to Bertha, waiting impatiently
for the parts to arrive—and learning for the first time that
Fetch and Krarup were on their way from San Francisco
in their Packard.

> *Ferris Hotel, Rawlins, Wyoming*
> *June 28, 1903.*
> *My darling Swipes,*
>   *Just a line to say that I am still alive. . . . Our*
> *things arrived this morning & we held divine services*
> *in the Blacksmith shop. We shall try & get away*
> *tonight. Our car will now be as good as new.*
>   *We have had hard luck, but I think it all came at*
> *once. We shall now try & make a record trip. The*
> *worst of it is over & everyone is congratulating us.*
>   *There are [others] on the way . . . trying to beat us*
> *across . . . [but] I feel confident they will give it up.*

With their car repaired, Jackson and Crocker headed
for Laramie and at Elk Mountain encountered some of
the steepest slopes of their journey—rocky trails in which
they sometimes had to jack up the car to get out of deep
ruts or stop to push boulders out of their path. In other

Elk Mountain, Wyoming ➤

Jackson fills the radiator tank with water.

places, ranchers were using the road as irrigation ditches, slowing the travelers down even more on the slippery surface. Seventeen times in one day the men resorted to the block and tackle to keep moving. "I never worked so hard in my life," Jackson told his wife, "but we can show what the machine & *good* men can do."

Along the way an old Wyoming rancher asked Jackson where they had come from. San Francisco, he was told.

Where were they headed? the man asked. New York, they replied.

"Where is your home?" he finally inquired, and when Jackson answered, "Vermont," the old man exclaimed, "What in *Hell* will you Vermonters do next?"

In Medicine Bow, an enterprising storekeeper learned just how badly they needed gasoline and made the most of it. Jackson was so outraged at the gouging that when he arrived in Laramie the next day, he complained about it to the local newspaper, the *Boomerang:*

Dr. Jackson . . . said that when he left Oregon the sheriff there warned him to beware of hold-ups, but that the only place he believed he had been held-up so far was at a place he believed they called Medicine Bow crossing between here and Rawlins where they charged him $5.25 for five gallons of gasoline.

East of Laramie they struck the best road they had traveled since California's Sacramento Valley, and they sped along on it to Cheyenne, where a large crowd gathered to gawk at what the Wyoming *Tribune* called a "Whizz Wagon." The *Tribune* also noted that Bud's "eyes are badly bloodshot from the exposure to alkali dust. It is to be doubted that he is enjoying the journey," the newspaper opined, "as he spends most of his time resting under the car."

The Inter Ocean Hotel
Cheyenne, Wyo.
July 1st, 1903.
Darling Swipes:

I have just shook hands & talked to 200 people & the only way I could get away was to say that I had a little wife at home that was expecting a letter from me. You don't know how glad I was to get your three dear letters. They put new vigor into me, you dear girl.

Form No. 1.
THE WESTERN UNION TELEGRAPH COMPANY.
INCORPORATED
23,000 OFFICES IN AMERICA. CABLE SERVICE TO ALL THE WORLD.

This Company TRANSMITS and DELIVERS messages only on conditions limiting its liability, which have been assented to by the sender of the following message.
Errors can be guarded against only by repeating a message back to the sending station for comparison, and the Company will not hold itself liable for errors or delays in transmission or delivery of Unrepeated Messages, beyond the amount of tolls paid thereon, nor in any case where the claim is not presented in writing within sixty days after the message is filed with the Company for transmission.
This is an UNREPEATED MESSAGE, and is delivered by request of the sender, under the conditions named above.
ROBERT C. CLOWRY, President and General Manager.

NUMBER ___ SENT BY ___ REC'D BY ___ 10 Paid CHECK Via Hillsdale Wyo. 803

RECEIVED at Burl Vt July 2 190 3
Dated Archer Wyo 2
To Mrs H Nelson Jackson

Fly wheel came off shaft held here for several days

H Nelson Jackson

Well the worst of our trip is over & everyone now says that we can make it & although there are [others] on the way _we will get there first_.

Just watch me now.
Nellie.

Behind lay the ramparts of the western mountains, the alkali deserts, and the sagebrush-choked broken terrain that had bedeviled and delayed them since late May. Ahead stretched the Great Plains and the farm country of the Midwest—gently undulating land that invitingly offered the prospect of a thousand miles of relatively straight, flat roads all the way to Chicago. "We will make up for lost time," Jackson promised his wife, "and you will see by my telegrams what time we are making."

But the first telegram he sent after leaving Cheyenne on the afternoon of July 2 told a different story: "Fly wheel came off shaft. Held here for several days."

Less than an hour out of Cheyenne, the stud bolts on the *other* connecting rod had broken off, and the *Vermont*

had ground to a dead stop. "Our feelings," Jackson wrote, "may be more easily imagined than described." A railroad grading crew towed the car to their camp near the small station of Archer. Crocker stripped the front seat off the car to get at the engine while Jackson wired the Winton factory once more for replacement parts—and once more settled in to wait for their delivery by train, day after agonizing day.

Sunday, July 5th, 1903.
My darling Swipes:

We expected our express on No. 5 at three this afternoon, but a message this noon from the train agent says that he has nothing, so it is another day. It has been an awful long time to us and I shall be mighty glad when we are on the way again.
I have sent with the order for everything I think we will need and unless another serious accident happens we ought to be able to make good time across these plains.

. . . We are camping out with a grade gang & eating with 15 men. The contractor has given us a bunk in one of the tents. Archer consists of the station & section house. On Friday afternoon we had snow.

A stripped-down **Vermont** *waits for parts.*

/>

We celebrated the 4th by sleeping & killing time. I sent in town for 2 kegs of beer so the men enjoyed themselves.

Well, tomorrow is our anniversary & I wish I could be with you. I want to celebrate here by getting my new parts. I shall think of you a good deal tomorrow, as I always do. You are the best little wife in the world and I am a mighty lucky fellow to have you.

Yes, old Girl, I appreciate it, if sometimes I have a queer way of showing it. Four years tomorrow!!!! They have been very short & dear ones to me. You have done everything in the world to make me happy.

I shall just tear up the ground until I can be with you. With lots of love to all I am yours.

P.S. I am not much of a hand to write love letters: you didn't give me a chance for much practice, but you know dear how I feel.

Separated from his wife by roughly two thousand miles, on July 6 Jackson marked their fourth anniversary with a brief telegram: "Many happy returns of the day and much love. Parts did not come today." But apparently he also had made arrangements via the telegraph for Bertha to receive a gift in his absence, because a few days later he dispatched a cryptic (and otherwise completely incomprehensible) message: "That is a pretty blue dress you have on this afternoon."

————————————

Jackson had now been on the road for forty-two days—nearly half of the ninety specified in his wager. But he was only a third of the way to New York, and his car now seemed to be breaking down at every turn. Even worse, with Tom Fetch and Marius Krarup and their Packard following a more direct route across the West, Jackson was concerned that they might be catching up with him.

They were.

Except for the day spent waiting for more film, Fetch and Krarup had been constantly on the move. The factory mechanic traveling with them had kept the car operating efficiently, and they were running right on schedule.

On July 3, they completed their second week of travel by covering 114 miles and reaching Promontory, Utah, where the golden spike joining the first transcontinental railroad had been driven in 1869.

And on July 4, after driving another 106 miles, they pulled into Salt Lake City to a wave of publicity—precisely what the company's advertising executive had planned. "So far they have had no accidents and have not been towed a foot," gushed the Salt Lake *Tribune*. "Their chief difficulty, in fact, has been the malice of rural guides, who several times have sent them off on the wrong roads."

At the rate they were going, despite starting nearly a month later, Fetch and Krarup were now only ten days behind Jackson and Crocker.

Complicating matters even more, on July 6 yet another automobile set off from San Francisco for New York. Lester Whitman and Eugene Hammond were driving a 1903 Oldsmobile runabout—the first automobile to be made on an assembly line, and the first that would outsell electric and steam-powered machines. It was smaller and cheaper than the two big touring cars that were already on the road.

Whitman and Hammond leave San Francisco.

But like the Packard expedition, this one was also underwritten by a manufacturer.

Ransom Olds himself had provided Whitman and Hammond—both experienced drivers and Oldsmobile mechanics—with the car, free tires, and the promise to reimburse their expenses and pay them a thousand-dollar bonus if they reached New York successfully.

Hoping to generate extra publicity for their trip, Whitman and Hammond picked up a letter from San Francisco's mayor and promised to carry it east and deliver it to the mayor of New York. Following the same route as Fetch and Krarup, they quickly crossed the Sierras and were well into Nevada within a week's time.

There were now three automobiles racing to become the first to cross the continent.

90

Whitman and Hammond en route to New York ➤

➤   ➤   ➤   ➤   ➤   ➤   ➤   ➤   ➤

CHAPTER SIX

BUFFALO WALLOWS

July 7th, 1903.
Western Union Telegraph
Company, Archer, Wyoming

To: Mrs. H. Nelson Jackson,
     Burlington, Vt.

Leave this noon. Parts arrived
last a.m. Now in good shape.
Hope to be with you soon.

                    H. Nelson Jackson

On July 7, with another five-day delay waiting for parts and repairs behind them, Jackson and Crocker were eagerly on their way again. Following an old military and stage route from Cheyenne to Julesburg, Colorado, they crossed the rolling grasslands into Nebraska, stopping briefly while a blacksmith repaired the front axle, which had broken along the way. At the Platte River, they once more began tracing the same route blazed by pioneer wagon trains heading for Oregon and California half a century earlier.

Nominally, the roads were improving as they moved eastward. But the summer of 1903 was turning into one of the wettest summers in memory—a "Second Flood," Jackson wrote Bertha, "rain, rain, rain, & plenty of mud"—and the roads had become quagmires.

When we crossed into Nebraska [the mud] became worse instead of better. Here it rained constantly. The mud was a cementlike mass that stuck to things like the best Portland. And it seemed to have no bottom.

CROSSING THE CONTINENT IN HEAVY AUTOMOBILE

Dr. H. Nelson Jackson, Wealthy Vermonter, Arrives in Omaha on His Way Back Home.

Declares His Trip Has Been Rather Expensive and Beset With Many Obstacles.

Dr. H. Nelson Jackson, who for ten years practiced medicine in Burlington, Vt., and then retired with a fortune, is making an automobile trip from San Francisco to his Vermont home. He has traveled 3,800 miles, and arrived in Omaha last night, putting his machine in charge of H. E. Frederickson for repairs. Dr. Jackson is not in the automobile business, nor in the advertising business, but is making the trip across the country for his own pleasure, and to prove to a party of friends that the

The car sank in it clear up to the battery boxes—that is, nearly to the tops of the wheels; and then we would get out the block and tackle and haul it out.

One day we repeated this performance eighteen times; other days it would be from three to eight times. These places were locally termed "buffalo wallows." We wallowed in them, sometimes tearing down a section of fence or using sage brushes where there were no fences, and put them under the wheels to make a foundation.

On their most frustrating day, they worked from six a.m. to midnight to make a mere sixteen miles. Covered with mud, Jackson stopped at a small homestead, hoping to buy food. "Perhaps I did look trampish when I knocked at the housewife's door," he later recalled, "but no sooner did I mention food than the door was slammed in my face, with the admonition, 'We don't give no hand-outs here.' "

They detoured north for a while, away from the Platte River, and ran along the edges of the Nebraska Sand Hills,

Stuck again: a farmer gets his horses ready.

Traffic control

picking up speed as they finally found better roads. They rushed through Kearney and Grand Island and dozens of smaller farm towns, and as the telegraph lines announced their impending arrival in each one, people flocked to see Jackson and his machine—not because an automobile was a novelty in this part of the country, but because of growing curiosity about whether Jackson was about to make history. "Disappointment was keen," one newspaper reported, "when he tore through the towns at a forty-mile [an hour] clip without stopping." The Columbus, Nebraska, *Telegram* told of an encounter that was even more disappointing:

> The collision of an automobile with a horse and carriage was a novel scene enacted on one of the main traveled roads west of Columbus last Saturday afternoon. Fred Lamp was in the carriage, and a pair of strangers were driving the automobile. The road in that vicinity runs parallel with the Union Pacific railroad. Mr. Lamp was driving a fractious horse; and for several minutes he had given the most of his attention to an approaching train behind him.
>
> He failed to see the automobile coming from the other direction until it was close upon him. Then he

turned quickly to the right as custom has established in passing teams on the public road, but the automobile turn[ed] in the same direction and the two vehicles came together. For a few minutes horse hair, cuss words and escaping

The Paxton
RALPH KITCHEN, MANAGER.
AMERICAN AND EUROPEAN PLAN.
Sunday night
Omaha Neb. 190
You naughty girl — I have lost six hours of valuable time

steam were flying through the air, and it was pretty hard to tell what kind of damage was going on.

Then the air cleared. Neither the occupants nor the vehicles were damaged seriously. Mr. Lamp and his horse drove away with a proud, defiant air, and after a while the automobilists made their getaway in a cloud of steam. The identity of the chauffeurs is still unknown.

It is believed they were a wealthy San Francisco doctor and his friend who are touring the continent in their horseless carriage.

In a final, long, nonstop effort in Nebraska, they covered an astonishing 265 miles, even though the front axle once more snapped in two. They borrowed a short piece of iron pipe from a farmer, hastily shoved the broken axle ends into it, wedged them in place with tire irons, drove another twenty miles until they found a blacksmith who welded things back together—and kept on moving through the night. ("Two bottles of Paine's Celery [Compound] pulled me through," Jackson joked in a telegram to Bertha to explain his endurance.)

On the morning of July 12, they rolled into Omaha, near the place where Lewis and Clark had held their first meeting with American Indians nearly a century earlier. Now, a huge crowd turned out to greet Jackson and *his* expedition.

The Paxton Hotel
Sunday night
You naughty girl—
I have lost six hours of valuable time reading your dear letters—when I ought to & want to work on my car so that I can be with you as soon as possible—but I can tell you I was d—— glad to get them. You

*The **Vermont** reaches Omaha.* ➤

*dear girl it did me a lot of good & made me a little
homesick.*

*. . . On our arrival here this morning we found half
of the city turned out. . . . I never thought a little
thing like what we have done could get up so much
interest, but I have received today bushells of
telegrams from all over congratulating me & the
whole city has had a piece each of my old shoes. Good
night old girl—Watch me now—more reporters down
stairs—yours till a widow.*

Nel.

By this point, Jackson had grown adept at giving inter-
views to newspaper reporters, and some of his adventures
(occasionally exaggerated or slightly modified for local
consumption) already were coalescing into an entertaining
and spellbinding narrative he delivered at each stop: the
improbable bet in San Francisco; the homesteaders cow-
ering under their wagon at the *Vermont's* approach; the
addition of Bud (on his way to becoming as much a
celebrity as Jackson himself); the kindly sheepherder's
meal after thirty-six foodless hours; the struggles with
"buffalo wallows" (a term the reporters seemed to love as
much as Jackson); and the "holdup" at Medicine Bow, a

More mud

story he told so well that no reporter could seemingly resist repeating it.

President Theodore Roosevelt—one of Jackson's personal heroes, who shared some of the same traits of limitless enthusiasm, can-do optimism, and chronic impulsiveness—had passed through Omaha in his special train earlier in the summer on a frenetic and wildly successful whistle-stop tour of the western states. As leader of the nation (and a master of press relations) Roosevelt had commanded much bigger crowds and larger headlines, but Jackson, who had by now also become accustomed to welcoming parties and a clutch of journalists scribbling down his pronouncements, could not resist comparing himself in some ways to the youthful president he so much admired. "Me & Pres Roosevelt has had quite a reception through the West," he exulted to Bertha in one letter; two days later, apparently still pleased with the thought, he told her the same thing again.

The *Omaha Morning World-Herald* emphasized Jackson's expenses as well as his adventures:

Dr. Jackson is not in the automobile business, nor in the advertising business, but is making the trip across the country for his own pleasure, and to prove to a party of friends that the trip can be made. In fact, it has proven quite an expensive luxury . . . for the repair bills have been enormous to say nothing of the other expenses.

. . . The experiences and adventures of the trip have been of an exciting nature, which may be better understood when it is known that he traveled 3,000 miles through a country never before touched by an automobile.

. . . Before leaving, the machine will have a thorough overhauling and be put into condition for fast running. Incidentally, half a ton of Nebraska clay, which it has gathered during the past few days, will be removed, and the car will be made more presentable.

The spreading news of Jackson's quest—as well as the heavy publicity surrounding both the Packard and the Oldsmobile journeys—had not only aroused greater public interest in the *Vermont*'s progress; it had spurred the Winton Company into action. A representative from the Cleveland office was waiting for him in Omaha with a surprising proposal: to make sure Jackson arrived in New York first, the Winton Company was willing to provide

102 him with the same financial and logistical support that the Oldsmobile and Packard companies were giving the other two expeditions.

For someone beset with so many mechanical delays and now openly complaining to every reporter about his mounting expenses, this must have been a tempting offer—though it would mean the trip would now become as much the Winton Company's as Jackson's.

That evening, in his letter to Bertha, Jackson revealed his answer: "I have informed them that we have made the trip so far without their assistance & thought that perhaps [we] two greenhorns could do the rest of it."

"Winton's man," he added proudly in a hasty telegram the next morning, as he pulled out of Omaha with Crocker and Bud, "cannot understand how we made it." Following the route of the Chicago & Northwestern Railroad and what would later be the Lincoln Highway, now U.S. Highway 30, they sped across Iowa and western Illinois in such a rush that Jackson didn't even pause long enough to send more telegrams to let Bertha mark their progress. "The constant rains made the roads very bad," Jackson would later tell a reporter, "but after the buffalo wallows they were child's play. A few inches of mud made little difference to us . . . and we seldom had to fall back on our faithful block and tackle."

"A huge automobile, manned by a couple of sphinx-like men, shot through Jefferson on Tuesday morning, halting long enough on the west side of the square to oil up and replenish the big gasoline tank," reported the Jefferson *Bee* in central Iowa:

It was a big, unwieldy machine, built low, had wide rubber tires that could pick up dust by the bucketful, and yet it could run like a greyhound. The men in charge were as begrimed as a couple of colliers, looked as if they had absorbed a sack of dirt externally, with more than a peck on the inside.

. . . The motorman was a dabster in his line, and could pretty nearly turn his machine round on a half dollar coin. They pulled out for the east in a cloud of dust, and made Grand Junction in a trifle over thirty minutes. They were not arrested for fast driving; no, "to cook your hare, first catch your hare."

For the first time on the entire trip, Jackson was finally stringing together consecutive days without mishaps, breakdowns, or delays—and he was regularly averaging nearly 150 miles per day, something he had boasted to reporters in California, Oregon, Idaho, and Wyoming that the *Vermont* was easily capable of, but until now had rarely achieved.

The Marshalltown, Iowa, *Reflector* considered Jackson and Crocker "both badly bronzed and sunburnt" from their days in the open car, "but [they] seemed to be enjoying their trip immensely." Farther east, the Clarence, Iowa, *Sun* noted they had passed through town in the evening "making good time" and presciently predicted that "the next few years will see many of these pass through here."

They crossed the Mississippi at Clinton, and four days after leaving Omaha pulled into Chicago, where Jackson proclaimed, "We have come to the conclusion that we can run our car over any road that a man can take a team of horses and a wagon, providing we can get traction."

"We were honored with receptions by city officials, automobile dealers and hero worshippers generally,"

Bud guards the car.

Jackson wrote, "but the one thought in our minds was to finish."

A caravan of automobile enthusiasts gathered to escort them out of Chicago the next day, but the depar-

104 ture had to be delayed. Bud was missing. "Bud had taken it into his head to see the city," according to one newspaper account, "and his owners and others chased him around for sometime before he could be found." Restored at last to his place of honor as "the most satisfied passenger," Bud sat in the front seat as the *Vermont* led the procession of cars to Hammond, Indiana, then continued east on its own, passing through LaPorte on its way to South Bend after darkness fell.

Another 150-mile day over rain-soaked roads brought them to Toledo,

A convoy of Wintons greets the **Vermont.**

Ohio, on July 19, where the Toledo *Times* reported, "The trip has not been a cheap one, as Dr. Jackson said last night that if anyone figured on making the trip he would advise them to figure out their expenses and multi-ply [that] by 20." Once more, Jackson recounted the familiar tales of his adventure; once more, Bud and his goggles and his alkali-reddened eyes featured heavily in the story.

As Jackson neared Cleveland, home of the Winton Motor Carriage Company, the firm's executives sensed an imminent public relations bonanza, even without their direct sponsorship. (In fact, they would soon realize that Jackson's independence from the company made his story all the more compelling—and his choice of a Winton that much more valuable as an endorsement for the vehicle.)

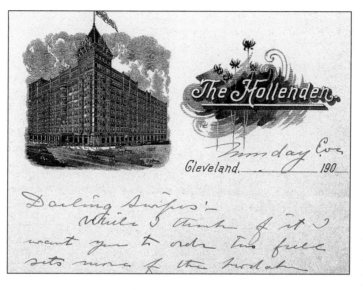

They wired Bertha an urgent telegram asking her to "rush special delivery all photographs" (which Jackson had been sending her from the road) and promised to return them "in good order." They stoked the local press into a frenzy—"Bold Chauffeur Due Today," one headline blazed; another called Jackson the "Daring Automobilist"; yet another referred to the "Hazardous Trip Supposed to Be Impossible." Bud, the Cleveland *Plain Dealer* advised its readers, was "so ugly that he is handsome."

On July 20—the fifty-ninth day of Jackson's journey—the Winton Company's advertising manager, Charles B. Shanks, who had accompanied Alexander Winton on his aborted transcontinental trip in 1901, led a convoy of cars to Elyria, Ohio, twenty-seven miles west of Cleveland, for a well-photographed personal handshake with the "continent-trotters." He then led them triumphantly into the city for a grand reception hosted by the Cleveland Automobile Club. According to *Motor Age* magazine:

> *The Jackson party left Chicago at noon Saturday and arrived in Cleveland at 5:00 p.m. Monday, remarkably good time for notoriously bad roads which had been rendered worse by continued hard rains.*
>
> *The party went to the Hollenden Hotel for a clean-up and for supper while the faithful bull dog mascot*

remained in charge and fought flies and kept off inquisitive newsboys.

In the evening the car was taken to the Winton garage and given a thorough cleaning. . . . Except for its heavy coat of mud and dilapidated front tires, the car is little the worse for its rough usage.

"When we started on this trip, my wife asked me how long it would take," Jackson told one of the many reporters who now hung on his every word. "I told her six weeks and possibly six months. I also told her that I would make the trip if it took a lifetime. I was positive that it could be done, and I have met with success where [Alexander] Winton and others failed." Sometime that evening, Bud was apparently released from guard duty long enough to sit (fully goggled) with Jackson and Crocker for a formal portrait for the next morning's paper.

———————

With only one state yet to go, Jackson was confident that this time the worst really was behind him, and he now believed that the other two expeditions could not possibly beat him to New York. It seemed like a safe bet. Despite their fast starts from San Francisco and all their meticulous planning, both expeditions had begun to run into problems of their own.

◄ *Surrounded in Cleveland*

WEEKLY   NEW YORK — SATURDAY, JULY 25, 1903 — CHICAGO   10 CENTS

Across America in an American Automobile.

Interesting Narrative of the Trip from the Summit of the Sierras across the Sage Brush and Heated Plains of Nevada — Arrival at Carson City creates greater Sensation than a Murder.

BY MARIUS C. KRARUP.

PRICE, Utah, July 9.—Too fagged for an early start after yesterday's exceedingly fatiguing travel along the south edge of the United Reservation and down to this point through Soldier Canyon, far famed for its roughness ; and with no suitable stopping place within reach by a half day's driving, we take a rest in the town, which is one of the mineral and shipping centers of the State of Utah, though the population does not exceed 700, and I find an opportunity to resume the description of our trip from where my account sent from Salt Lake City left us ; namely, at the summit of the Sierras in California at 10 o'clock Wednesday, June 24, on the point of descending to Lake Valley where the boundary of the State of Nevada cuts in from southeast to northwest till arrested by the shore of Lake Tahoe.

What the car—Old Pacific or "Pac."

OVER MOUNTAIN ROADS, SAGE BRUSH TRAILS AND SHIFTING STREAMS THE TRANSCONTINENTALISTS DRIVE ONWARD.

Special sand tires for the Oldsmobile

The Packard gets stuck in Utah

In Salt Lake City, Tom Fetch and Marius Krarup's car had been seized by a local sheriff because of a lawsuit filed against the Packard Company by a disgruntled ex-employee. After two days, the company posted a five-thousand-dollar bond, and the expedition was under way once more.

But instead of continuing along the direct route of the transcontinental railroad, Fetch and Krarup turned south-east, into the canyons of Utah and the heart of Colorado's Rocky Mountains—a route preselected for them by Packard's advertising director back in the East. "Like a dumb fool, I was thinking from the standpoint of pub-licity, with pictures of mountains and canyons," he said later, "but what I sent them into was something terrific."

They damaged an axle going through the difficult Wasatch Mountains, fractured a ball joint going through Castle Valley, got stuck trying to ford the Price River. In Colorado, rain made the roads so greasy they wrapped the tires with steel chains as they slowly wound their way through the Rockies.

When they finally reached Denver on July 20, a pro-cession of cars, with horns blaring, led them into the city like "a drove of cattle," according to the local newspaper, and the townspeople greeted them like heroes. But Fetch

and Krarup were now 1,300 miles behind Jackson, and New York City, they estimated, was still five weeks away.

The Oldsmobile runabout was even farther from its goal. To help them get through the Nevada deserts, Lester Whitman and Eugene Hammond had brought along special "sand tires" they had made themselves—canvas strips stuffed with cotton rags that kept the

Fetch and Krarup draw a crowd.

back wheels from sinking down in the deep drifts. But the car's chain-drive was so severely damaged climbing a hill, that they lost several days of progress—first finding a horse-and-wagon to tow their car to a railroad station, then losing another day when the replacement parts that arrived were the wrong ones, and they had to make temporary repairs at a blacksmith shop. More breakdowns plagued them—a damaged piston, then a broken part that allowed them to drive in reverse, but not forward.

On July 20, while Whitman and Hammond were in the midst of a three-day delay, waiting for more parts to arrive in Elko, Nevada, Jackson was two thousand miles farther east, excitedly writing his wife from Cleveland in preparation for the final leg of his journey.

The Hollenden
Monday Eve
Darling Swipes:
Well old girl I have brought the car to its birthplace & a great reception it got. The Pres of the firm with his associates came out & we had quite a procession into the city. They are all like a lot of kids.
. . . The car is at the shop & they are to work all night so that I can get away in the morning— I go from here to Buffalo. I am tired & got to get up early in the morning & damn anxious to get you in my arms.
Nel.

CHAPTER SEVEN

WATCH
ME NOW

Darling Swipes:
While I think of it I want you to order two full sets more of the Kodak pictures & have one set sent to Mrs. B. D. Crocker, Tacoma, Wash. Keep the other set for me & bring all pictures & photos to N.Y. when you come to meet me there— that is if you care to come.

. . . I have made arrangements to have the Winton agent at New York to take you up the Hudson to meet me. When I telegraph you to come down leave on the first train, telephone the agency you are at the Holland & I will telegraph you both [to] then come.

. . . Watch me now come to you.

Nel.

Jackson set off from Cleveland with Crocker and Bud on July 21, intent on reaching New York City as quickly as possible. To avoid the risk of crossing Pennsylvania's Allegheny Mountains, he decided to turn northeast, along the Great Lakes, to Buffalo, then to Albany on a new state road, before turning south again to follow the Hudson into Manhattan. It would add several hundred miles to the trip, but, as Jackson told a reporter, "we have had enough of mountains."

Ready for the final stretch

They quickly covered the two hundred miles to Buffalo, despite rains so fierce that Jackson telegraphed the Winton company: "If it continues, will ask you to send paddles for the wheels and rudder for the rear of car. May have to take out navigation papers." The *Vermont*, he told a reporter, was now splattered with samples of mud from every state they had crossed, and he didn't intend to wash any of it off until the trip was finished.

Running on roads that paralleled the old Erie Canal, they pushed on across New York state— sometimes driving well into the night, simply to put more miles behind them. He was sure he could make it to New York City in a matter of days, win his bet, and become the first person to drive across the continent— unless the *Vermont* broke down completely. Then the unthinkable happened.

East of Buffalo occurred the only real accident of our trip. Traveling in high—at least twenty miles an hour—the machine struck a hidden obstruction in the road. Crocker, Bud, and myself were thrown high in the air. Both mud-guards were torn off and the machine otherwise damaged.

Miraculously, none of them was hurt. And the *Vermont* was bruised, but, to everyone's relief, still able to run. They

116 drove on through Rochester, then Syracuse and Utica. After a night's rest in Little Falls, with the skies cloudless for the first time in weeks, they decided to take advantage of the break in the weather and drive the final 230 miles without stopping.

They rolled through Schenectady, crossed the Hudson at Albany and turned south on the Albany Post Road along the east bank of the river. News of their approach brought out cheering crowds as they passed through the towns of Hudson and Poughkeepsie. Night fell. On they went.

In Peekskill they delayed to patch a punctured tire by the glow of a hotel's outside light. There, Jackson's wife met him, along with a delegation of reporters and Winton Company officials, who hailed Jackson as "the automobile Pathfinder" and bedecked the *Vermont* with a banner that was inscribed, "First Across the Continent—San Francisco to New York." Then the small cavalcade motored south for the final miles without incident, except for a brief moment of confusion when it was discovered that a sleepy Bud had jumped into the wrong car. (He was awakened by a sharp command from his master and restored to his rightful place in the front seat of the *Vermont*.)

At 4:30 in the morning on Sunday, July 26, they crossed the Harlem River into Manhattan, drove down a quiet

Into the night

New York at dawn

Fifth Avenue, nearly deserted because of the early hour, and honked their horn to awaken the night porter at the Holland House hotel at Thirtieth Street.

Jackson had made it from San Francisco in 63 days, 12 hours, and 30 minutes—well within his wager of ninety days. And having become the first to drive a car across the nation, within hours of their entrance into New York, he and Crocker and Bud were the toast of the town. The New York *Herald* reported:

Dr. H. Nelson Jackson and Sewall K. Crocker, his chauffeur, finished the first transcontinental automobile trip at half-past four o'clock yesterday morning.

On their arrival, the mud besmirched and travel stained vehicle which had borne them so faithfully and sturdily over fifty-six hundred miles of roads between the Pacific and the Atlantic was housed in a garage in West 58th Street. All day yesterday it was visited by admiring automobilists, and curious passersby peeped in upon it. In honor of its achievement it was decorated with tiny flags and draped with national standards.

The thick coating of mud gave evidence that it had been somewhere and that somewhere a long way off. A broken mud guard and a sprung front axle alone attested the hard knocks it had had on its long journey.

For the next four days, a parade of reporters marched in and out of the Jacksons' suite at the Holland House to interview the "automobile Pathfinder" about his "thrilling dash over roadless country," as newspapers all across the nation told and retold Jackson's story, sometimes embellishing details—including one report that claimed the *Vermont* had floated across rivers, using its revolving wheels as propellers.

Jackson was described as a "sturdy, blue-eyed giant" who had lost twenty pounds from the rigors of his journey. (Roosevelt, on the other hand, having been feted with lavish banquets at every stop and constantly pampered en route by a personal chef on his presidential train, had complained about *gaining* seventeen pounds during his cross-country trip.) Bud—with and without his goggles— was a news photographer's dream come true, although one newspaper reported that he was "not accepting visitors." Crocker was always mentioned in the newspaper accounts (often with Jackson's heartfelt appreciation for being essential to the trip's success) but never quoted directly.

A proud display of mud and flags ➤

machinists re-
-t is said, will
men held in re-
-citement about
The scale calls
nt.

OTHERS.

unaways—
s Nose.

s yesterday in
-aways.
he East Fifty-
n Fifth-ave.
y-second sts.,
d to a buggy
e Joseph Par-
the Metropoli-
-and Charles
spirited gray
-ed into Fifth-

st, the horse
-tomobile and
driving, suc-
-until the bit
l, and he sped
ce. At Fifty-
-waving their
-ies' head was
and made a
n by the nos-
-his feet, and
-lyan got his
-and held on.
-alf before the
the policeman
Fifty-first-st.
-ed the patrol-
-is companion
-ie street was
the policeman

of the West
-opped a run-
Eight-ave. in
-jured.
-d to a coach
-o. 509 West
n, by James
-th-st. Doyle
horses stand-
-o mount the
-k flight and
speed. The

DR. J. N. JACKSON AND DOG BUD.
Who crossed the continent in automobile, wearing goggles.
(Photograph by Davis & Sanford.)

Dr. H. Nelson Jackson, of Burlington, Vt., who made the first automobile trip across this continent, had, besides his driver, a faithful companion in his bulldog, Bud. Bud stood the two months' journey well, and apparently en- joyed it. The only trouble he experienced was with his eyes, which, after a short time on the road, began to fail him. A pair of automobile goggles were made for him, and after that the dog had no further discomfort.

UNION MEN MOB DRIVER.

RESERVES CALLED OUT.

Nearly 800 Employes of N. Y. Transfer Company on Strike.

HIRED BY LAMAR, HE SAYS

NOT AT LONG BRANCH.

McClusky Declares He Has Evi- dence Against Broker.

ACCUS

New-Roch
Mayo

With an upli-
-lon, a promine-
County, disper-
his political ac-
sidewalk oppos-
Rochelle. He
an alderman a
Rochelle Pres-
that Dillon's
College, Fordi-
made a pass
about 325 poun-
two blocks.

The attack
factional fight
G. Agar, a w-
set out to ref-
who was forn-
now with Aga-
house and hol-
feeling betwee-
-lowers is bitte-
-ple have made-
-meeting across
-ig disparagin-
that they rav-
sitting on his
which the Boa-
house as a m-
that he has a-
his visits to th-
of talk was g-
could stand it
Smith to desis-
-hit Smith.

The editor s-
no talk derog-
of the latter's
friends were ta-
and were not a
he suddenly a-
-and said: "Co
Dillon, Smith
and wound up
which he had
Smith to Aga-
have authoriz-
Democratic Co
he would neit-
copy, and the
him.

GASOLE

In a Few
—His

Orange, N.
this afternoon
view on his
returned from
Mr. Edison

TRANS-CONTINENT AUTOISTS AND SOME SCENES
IN THEIR TRIP OF SIX THOUSAND MILES.

Dr. H. NELSON JACKSON.   S.E. WALL R. CROCKER.

"BUD."

GIVING RANCH CHILDREN A RIDE.

HOW THE CAMPING OUTFIT WAS PACKED.

ON THE CREN PRAIRIE.

DRY RIVER BED FOR A ROAD.

A ROCKY ROAD.

AUTO TRIP 'CROSS CONTINENT ENDS.

Dr. Jackson Tells of His Adventures on the 6,000-Mile Journey.

TOOK 63 DAYS, BUT ON 19 THEY DID NOT RUN

Machine Drew Itself from Bogs with Tackle and Swam Streams— Few Mishaps Suffered.

Dr. H. Nelson Jackson, of Burlington, Va., and Sewall R. Crocker, his chauffeur, completed at 4 o'clock yesterday morning an automobile trip across the continent, which began in San Francisco May 23. Their goal was the Holland House, at Thirtieth street and Fifth avenue.

It is the first time that an automobile has made the trip from ocean to ocean. A bulldog named Bud, which Dr. Jackson picked up in Idaho, made the journey to New York with him.

It was a battered old machine of disreputable appearance that startled the sleepy night porter at the Holland about the time the milk wagons were going their rounds. The body and running gear were scratched and battered and covered with mud, and the guard over one of the rear wheels had been carried away entirely. The tonneau was filled with luggage and an extra tire.

Dr. Jackson and Chauffeur Crocker wore canvas suits and caps which showed signs of rough usage. Their faces were bronzed to the shade of saddle leather. Physically they looked very fit.

Joyous Tooting of Horns.

The tourists were accompanied during the last few hours of their journey by the wife of Dr. Jackson, Harry Foedick, of Boston, and J. F. Horeau, of this city, who took a run up the Hudson in an auto to a point beyond Fishkill to meet them. There was a joyous tooting of horns when the Holland House was reached. Dr. Jackson's father, who is an Episcopal clergyman, was waiting there to meet him.

At his apartments in the Holland House yesterday afternoon Dr. Jackson gave an account of his adventures. "The trip had its origin," he said, "in

KEARSARGE ENDS HER DASH ACROSS OCEAN.

(Continued from First Page.)

Portsmouth took especial pains to see that

men have worked admirably, and the strain on them has been very great. The men in every grade have done their duty, and we are all proud of the ship." The officers and men on the Kearsarge

the ship did not meet the Dons until the battle of Santiago.

GIRL'S SLEEP MADE LOTS OF EXCITEMENT

Relatives, Friends, Boat Cap

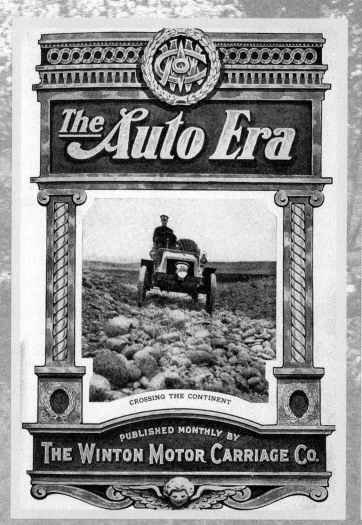

The Auto Era

CROSSING THE CONTINENT

PUBLISHED MONTHLY BY
THE WINTON MOTOR CARRIAGE CO.

The Auto Era

"I crossed the Continent in a Winton with Dr. H. Nelson Jackson"

PUBLISHED MONTHLY BY
THE WINTON MOTOR CARRIAGE CO.

One reporter noted that Bertha, "a sweet-faced brunette, who had approved of and urged the transcontinental attempt, could not resist the temptation to peep occasionally from an adjoining apartment to add a bit of information and comment to the recital of the journey's detail." She had brought along the letters and telegrams her husband had dispatched from the road; Jackson's father, the Reverend Samuel N. Jackson, was also on hand with newspaper clippings his son had sent him.

Jackson seems to have thrived on all the attention being lavished upon him—with one exception. A stylishly dressed woman sent her card to his room, saying she represented a New York newspaper. But when Jackson let her in, she promptly served him with a court summons—a complaint from a local dressmaker claiming nonpayment of $1,360 (perhaps the anniversary present Jackson had ordered via the telegraph from Wyoming). When asked about it by a reporter, for the first time on his trip Jackson had no comment. (He later said it was an unjust claim, and its disposition is unknown.)

In all, Jackson estimated that he had spent eight thousand dollars of his own money on the trip—the price of the car, a salary for Crocker, food and lodging, the seemingly endless need for new tires and replacement parts, eight hundred gallons of gasoline, and the fifteen dollars to purchase Bud. But, he said later, "It was worth every cent and every pound to win that fifty-dollar bet." In later years, different journalists would report different accounts about collecting his winnings—some quoting Jackson as saying he never got his money, and others saying that he did. His granddaughters, however, vividly recall how he distinguished the issue: he "won" the bet, he told them, but he never collected the money.

———————

Before leaving New York, Jackson wrote a long letter to the Winton Company describing his journey in their automobile. Eager to squeeze the maximum publicity possible out of his trip, the company quickly published the letter—with a raft of his photographs—in their publication *The Auto Era*. They also began running large advertisements in trade publications, calling their touring car's achievement "without parallel in American automobile history" and, ironically, making the most of the fact that before starting the trip Jackson "consulted neither manufacturer or sales agent." His vehicle "was not a specially constructed car. . . . The men who occupied the seats were not selected factory mechanics who had spent weeks and months in preparation . . . [and] there was no elaborate system of relays for duplicate parts, new tires and general supplies."

TRIUMPHANT

Dr. H. NELSON JACKSON, one of the best known surgeons in the country, accompanied by Mr. Sewall K. Croker, has completed his great trans-continental ride. This now distinguished automobilist, who is in no way connected with the automobile industry, undertook the ocean to ocean ride as a means of recreation and pleasure.

Dr. Jackson drove a regular model Winton car, purchased by him from a private owner in San Francisco, at a premium over the regular purchase price of $2,500. When he arrived in Cleveland (only 700 miles from New York) the motor was in such splendid condition that he refused to let it go into the Winton factory for a "looking over." It had gone up and over the High Sierras, traversed the Great Desert (a feat never accomplished by another automobile), climbed the rugged ascents and threaded the dangerous passes of the Rocky Mountains, rolled over the plains of Nebraska, ploughed through the black mud roads of Iowa and continued on through Illinois, Indiana and Ohio, but the motor was in such condition when Cleveland was reached that no factory inspection was necessary.

This record is the more remarkable when it is considered that no factory mechanic accompanied Dr. Jackson, and that he had no system of relays for duplicate parts, tires or other supplies along the route.

DR. JACKSON AT THE WHEEL.

Upon leaving San Francisco he carried but one extra tire, four extra spark plugs, a shovel, an axe, a cooking and camping outfit and a bulldog.

Dr. Jackson left San Francisco May 23d, going north through the picturesque Oregon country, and thence east over the Great Desert, arriving in New York July 26, having made a total mileage of about 6,000 miles, at an average speed of over 100 miles per day, although the Doctor made no attempt at a speed record.

―――――

If you are interested in America's Standard Highest Grade Car, send for catalog.

―――――

THE WINTON MOTOR CARRIAGE CO.

Factories and Head Office, CLEVELAND, U. S. A.

When rumors later surfaced that perhaps Jackson had actually driven two vehicles, or that he shipped his car across part of the West via railroad (some suspected the Packard Company as the rumor's source), the Winton Company immediately publicized a ten-thousand-dollar reward "to anyone who could produce the slightest evidence showing the truth in any of the various malicious stories." Angered that his own honor had been challenged, Jackson personally added fifteen thousand dollars to the company's pot. No one ever came forward. And in the end—based largely on the local newspaper clippings Jackson had collected in one small town after another, and on the letters and telegrams Bertha had saved—the major automotive press soon declared that Jackson's journey was authentically the first automobile trip across the nation.

On Thursday, July 30, Jackson and his wife, with Bud on board, headed home together in the *Vermont*. The trip took a week, and was punctuated by the problems and delays he had become accustomed to by now. The low-speed clutch broke in Hudson, then the high-speed clutch gave out in Albany, and a breaker box failed in Middlebury, Vermont. Near Shelburne, Jackson's two brothers showed up in their own automobile to escort him and Bertha the final ten miles. But a cylinder blew out in *their* car, so Jackson chained it to the *Vermont* and towed them the rest of the way into Burlington.

At last, on the late afternoon of August 7, he reached his home on the corner of Willard and Main Streets and went to park his trusted car in the stable. Just as the *Vermont* crossed the threshold, its drive chain—one of the few parts that had made the entire journey without a problem—snapped in two.

Two weeks later, Tom Fetch and Marius Krarup and their Packard finally made it to New York City, having completed their trip in a day and a half less than Jackson's time, but finishing second nonetheless. They were escorted into the city by a host of Packards and greeted by a cheering crowd. "Thank the Lord," one of them said as he got out of the car, "it's over."

On September 17, Lester Whitman and Eugene Hammond reached New York in their small Oldsmobile runabout (total time: 72 days, 21 hours, and 30 minutes). In a

Whitman and Hammond reach Boston.

festive ceremony at City Hall, they finally delivered the grease- and water-stained letter they had carried all the way from San Francisco's mayor. And in a gimmick to gain greater publicity for their company, Whitman and Hammond then drove up the coast to Boston, where they dipped the Oldsmobile's front wheels into the Atlantic— and claimed to be the first true "sea-to-sea" drivers.

Meanwhile, back home in Vermont, Jackson soon had *his* car up and running again, as a clipping from a local newspaper clearly attests:

October 3rd, 1903. Dr. H.N. Jackson, first man to cross the continent in an automobile was arrested in Burlington, Vermont, and fined [five dollars, plus court costs] for driving the machine more than six miles an hour.

Burlington, Vermont ➤

CHAPTER EIGHT

A SIGNAL TRIUMPH

The old pioneer days are gone, with their roughness and their hardship, their incredible toil and their wild, half-savage romance. But the need for the pioneer virtues remains the same as ever.

. . . We have every right to take a just pride in the great deeds of our forefathers; but we show ourselves unworthy to be their descendants if we make what they did an excuse for our lying supine instead of an incentive to the effort to show ourselves, by our acts, worthy of them.

. . . Now, in 1903, in the altered conditions, we must meet the changed and changing problems with the spirit shown by the men who, in 1803, and in the subsequent years gained, explored, conquered, and settled this vast territory, then a desert, now filled with thriving and populous States.
—Theodore Roosevelt, speech at the dedication of the Louisiana Purchase Exposition, St. Louis, Missouri

In 1903, as the nation began celebrating one hundred years of growth and expansion since the Louisiana Purchase and Lewis and Clark's epic voyage across the continent, Americans sensed that their world had suddenly got much smaller.

In 1903, President Theodore Roosevelt sent a New Year's greeting to England's King Edward VII using Marconi's new wireless radio that could transmit signals across the Atlantic.

On the Lincoln Highway

In 1903, a cable was laid across the Pacific Ocean, the last link in a web of wires that allowed Roosevelt to telegraph the first message sent around the world. The complete circuit took twelve minutes.

In 1903, the Trans-Siberian railroad was completed; and, with the active encouragement of the United States, Panama declared its independence from Colombia in order to pave the way for a canal to be built between the two great oceans.

In 1903, George A. Wyman made the first transcontinental motorcycle trip, bumping along much of the route from San Francisco to New York City by riding on the railroad bed.

In 1903, two bicycle mechanics from Dayton, Ohio, named Orville and Wilbur Wright, made the world's first airplane flight—soaring in their gasoline-powered machine over the beaches at Kitty Hawk, North Carolina. And farther down the coast that same year, Alexander Winton

◀ *Make way for a new century.*

drove one of his cars an astonishing sixty-eight miles per hour on Daytona Beach.

To the Boston *Herald*, Jackson's achievement seemed particularly significant:

What is admitted to be the greatest automobile performance of the year was the transcontinental tour of Dr. H. Nelson Jackson and his chauffeur, from San Francisco to New York. . . . The trip is considered as a signal triumph for the comparatively new means of travel.

It was one that would test the powers of endurance of a railway express locomotive to run an average of 12 hours everyday for two full months, but this is the feat performed by the automobile which carried [them].

The journey was made purely for pleasure and to satisfy an enthusiastic motorist that it could be accomplished. But it has demonstrated much more than this. It has shown the possibilities of the automobile, even with the generally disreputable highways which are characteristic of nearly every rural district in the country.

But when good roads shall be the rule, instead of the exception, in every state, it may be predicted with confidence that such journeys as that made by Dr. Jackson will be far from extraordinary.

Within a few years of Jackson and Crocker's trip, an organized movement began in the United States to improve the nation's roads to accommodate the automobile—to provide better surfaces, better maps, better ways for people in cars to travel wherever they wished to go. A new century was unfolding in which the automobile—for better and for worse—would completely transform American life. Just as Jackson had predicted in San Francisco, cars turned out to be much more than a "passing mechanical fancy" or an "unreliable novelty" suitable only for short distances—and an entire nation was about to "succumb completely to a primary enthusiasm" for motoring, just as he had.

In 1904, an automobile would be driven across the continent in half of Jackson's time; two years later, the time was cut in half once more.

In 1908, Jacob Murdock loaded his wife and children into his new Packard Model Thirty, and drove from Pasadena to New York City in 32 days—becoming the first family to drive across the country, and beginning a tradition of road trips that generations of American families would follow. Murdock refused to let anyone else behind

Murdock family trip: "Are we there yet?" ➤

Road grading

Preparing the roadbed

Rolling a new surface

the wheel, didn't like to ask for directions, and some days   139
kept on the move for more than twelve straight hours in
order to put some extra miles behind him. "I know nothing
more disheartening," he said, "than to see the sun just
about to set below the horizon, when one is many miles
from the place he had hoped to make that day."

By 1913, the nation's first transcontinental motor
route—the Lincoln Highway—had been created across
the center of the country. And by 1916, an automobile had
raced across its entire length in just five days' time.

Sewall Crocker did not live long enough to see that day.
Immediately after his and Jackson's journey in 1903, he
had stayed in New York, negotiating with a newspaper to
sponsor him on a six-month automobile expedition around
the world. Nothing ever came of it. But he did eventually
make a two-year tour of Europe, before being called back
to look after some family property in Mexico during that
country's revolution. Crocker suffered a nervous breakdown from the strain, took ill, and died in his hometown of
Tacoma on April 22, 1913.

By all accounts, Bud apparently lived a full dog's life,
content to guard the Jackson home in Vermont and take
short automobile trips around Burlington with his master.
Following Bud's death, the Jacksons always kept at least

The Lincoln Highway in Pennsylvania

one dog in their house, though none ever became as celebrated as the begoggled bull pup who had crossed the continent.

The Winton Motor Carriage Company (later renamed the Winton Motor Car Company, then, more succinctly, the Winton Company) rode the waves of publicity surrounding Jackson's trip for as long as it could. But its heavier, higher-priced touring cars were soon outsold by the smaller, cheaper models (like the Oldsmobile runabout) that began dominating the market once everyday Americans started buying cars of their own. The company produced its last automobiles in 1924.

Horatio Nelson Jackson, meanwhile, never stopped moving forward. In Burlington, he became a successful businessman—newspaper publisher, owner of the town's first radio station, president of a bank. Already in his mid-forties when World War I broke out, he insisted on enlisting in the Army despite his age (even arranged a personal meeting with an aging Theodore Roosevelt to seek the ex-president's intercession on his behalf). At war's end, he

The Jackson family, 1919

returned from overseas a decorated hero, having received the Distinguished Service Cross as well as France's Croix de Guerre. Back in the United States, he helped found the American Legion and later ran unsuccessfully for governor of Vermont.

In 1944, to preserve his moment in history, Jackson donated his car (as well as his scrapbook of newspaper clippings and Bud's goggles) to the Smithsonian Institution in Washington, D.C. And for the rest of his life he never tired of telling anyone who would listen the story of his great adventure crossing the continent with Sewall Crocker and the bulldog, Bud, in a 1903 Winton called the *Vermont*.

By the time Jackson died at age eighty-two—on January 14, 1955—his nation had already begun planning an interstate highway system, a series of roads that would soon routinely carry millions of cars and trucks from coast to coast, moving at such speeds and in such comfort that someone traveling them would find it nearly impossible to imagine *anything* like Horatio's drive.

One last spin: Jackson and the Vermont, *1944* ➤

SONG OF THE OPEN ROAD

Afoot and light-hearted, I take to the open road,
Healthy, free, the world before me,
The long brown path before me, leading wherever I
*   choose.*
Henceforth I ask not good-fortune—I myself am good
*   fortune;*
Henceforth I whimper no more, postpone no more, need
*   nothing,*
Strong and content, I travel the open road.
                                        —Walt Whitman

Much of the last twenty years of my life has been spent traveling America. I've retraced the entire length of the Lewis and Clark trail four times (in an old Saab, an even older Volkswagen bus, and twice in borrowed Suburbans). Another time, researching a book about the most sparsely populated counties in the United States, I drove thirty thousand miles in twelve months, crisscrossing the West. Scouting for stories and scenic locations for a documentary film series two years later, I crisscrossed the West again.

I once went by bus from Keene, New Hampshire, to Keene, California, and back on a thirty-day Greyhound pass, realizing by Day Two that such a trip might make an interesting magazine story but that there's good reason why the only people who use the bus for long-distance travel are those without any other option. I took the train from New England to the Midwest and back during midwinter, trying to sleep in one coach that had no heat and then in another that was swelteringly hot; by the time the return train delivered me home, exactly twenty-four hours behind schedule, I had concluded that most long-distance train travelers were either another sub-category of riders without options, phobic about flying, or blindly nostalgic about railroads. And having worked for two failed presidential campaigns, I've flown into and out of every airport in every American city big enough to have a television station, ridden countless miles in Secret Service–protected motorcades, and witnessed photo ops involving every possible mode of transportation, from tugboats to tanks. (I took a pass on the chance to ride in the tank, a choice the candidate later wished he had made as well.)

I've traveled the rodeo circuit with cowboys who saw nothing unusual about driving thousands of miles—nonstop for two days—for the chance to ride a wild bronc for eight seconds, and then set off for the next rodeo a thousand miles farther down the road. I've climbed into the cabs of 18-wheelers to explore the bizarre life of long-haul truckers, who inhabit a parallel universe from the rest of us, an unending paid-by-the-mile existence confined to interstates and truck stops that makes it possible for a head of Boston lettuce to be harvested in Yuma, Arizona, one morning and consumed in Boston four days later. Most recently, following the route of Horatio Nelson Jackson and his historic 1903 automobile trip from San Francisco to New York City, I drove more than ten thousand meandering miles in six weeks.

That was for work. For fun, what I enjoy the most is taking my family on long car trips. If my wife, daughter, or son aren't available, I've got good friends with a similar taste for the road as myself. And if *they* can't make it . . . well, there's nothing like some time alone behind the wheel to unwind from the stress and strain of jobs and close relationships.

You road I enter upon and look around! I believe you are not all that is here,
I believe that much unseen is also here.

Having revealed my predilections in the spirit of full disclosure, to state now that I believe one of the defining characteristics of Americans is an unquenchable restlessness, an itch to see what's over the next horizon, might seem a solipsism—defining my countrymen by what most clearly applies to me. But I believe it nonetheless. And I'm bolstered in this belief by finding myself in good company.

From Walt Whitman to Jack Kerouac, our bards have taken to the open road—to find inspiration, to discover themselves and their country, and in turn to reveal us to ourselves. Even Robert Frost, who might not immediately come to mind in the literature of travel (unless you count his move from New Hampshire to Vermont), acknowledged the central fact of movement to the national experience during the crowning moment of his career, when he became the first poet ever invited to speak at a presidential inauguration, John F.

Useful information on the Lincoln Highway

Kennedy's, and intoned that we Americans had not found our essence until "we gave ourselves outright/To the land vaguely realizing westward." (JFK, in turn, declared a New Frontier and spurred his nation toward it.)

For Mark Twain, arguably *the* representative American, at least in the eyes of the rest of the world, restlessness became a way of life. "All I do know or feel," he wrote his mother from California as a young man hungry for success, "is that I am wild with impatience to move—move—*move! . . .* I wish I never had to stop anywhere for a month." It was through his first travel books, *The Innocents Abroad* and *Roughing It,* that he first achieved the success he craved. It was through *Adventures of Huckleberry Finn,* his classic "road trip" novel (even if Huck and Jim's highway was the Mississippi River), that he achieved immortality.

Willie Nelson's theme song is "On the Road Again." Bruce Springsteen's is "Thunder Road." One generation believed you could "get your kicks on Route 66," while the next were reminded, through *Easy Rider* and *Thelma and Louise,* that not all road trips end quite so happily. *Lonesome Dove,* the Pulitzer Prize–winning novel by Larry McMurtry that became a television sensation, is an epic road-trip-in-buckskins in which a large cast of characters travels a straight (though arduous) line from Texas to Montana; *Blue Highways,* the

best-seller by my friend William Least Heat-Moon, is a solo journey that circles the nation.

I'm not suggesting that all these works—and the innumerable others like them—created a national psychology of road fever. In fact, I'm arguing just the opposite. They have endured because, like all great works of art (and in Kennedy's case, great political leadership), they resonated in perfect pitch with our national experience—as if we were a diverse array of tuning forks which, if struck just right, begins vibrating in unison the Song of the Open Road, the anthem of our collective history.

> *From this hour, freedom!*
> *From this hour I ordain myself loos'd of limits and imaginary lines,*
> *Going where I list, my own master, total and absolute,*
> . . . .
> *I inhale great draughts of space;*
> *The east and the west are mine, and the north and the south are mine.*

The first refrains were sung long before we were a nation. When Europeans began arriving in North America more than five hundred years ago, they brought with them many things that proved disastrous to Native Americans—most notably, deadly diseases that quickly spread from tribe to tribe, devastating even those who had never even seen a white man, and a cultural desire to spread across and take over the Indians' land. But the Europeans also brought something that many western tribes considered so wondrously beneficial that they named it the "sacred dog" and totally rearranged their lives around it. It was the horse.

Following the Pueblo Revolt of 1680, the horses that the retreating Spanish left behind in New Mexico began spreading throughout the West, transforming each tribe they reached. Almost immediately, a new world opened for people who had relied on their feet to trek great distances and on their dogs to drag their meagre belongings. Buffalo were now easier to hunt (and could be followed deeper into the Great Plains). Teepees were now easier to move (and could be made larger to hold more possessions). Enemies were easier to reach and raid (and horses were the prime booty). Wealth and status were measured by the size of a family's horse herd (and during winter, a man's prized stallion would be staked inside the family's lodge to protect it from the cold). No tribe was unaffected. Some—including the Cheyenne—gave themselves over to the horse entirely, abandoning their fields and permanent villages to take on the life of nomadic

A culture transformed by the horse

hunters. West of the Mississippi, the revolution wrought by the horse was so complete and so sudden that within only a few generations, elders would tell their disbelieving grandchildren tales of life back in the "dog days."

It was almost as if, in the limitless spaces at the heart of the New World, the native people had been waiting to receive this beast from the Old World, adopt it overnight, and through it attain some higher expression of their spirit—proud, free, and mobile. The Cheyenne, in fact, say they *had* been waiting. According to their stories, their great prophet Sweet Medicine had prepared them in advance. "This animal will carry you on his back and help you in many ways," he had promised his people, long before the Cheyenne had heard of horses or white men. "Those far hills that seem only a blue vision in the distance take many days to reach now; but with this animal you can get there in a short time, so fear him not." Other Native Americans like to point out that the first horse on earth originated in America and became extinct in its homeland at the end of the Pleistocene, though some of its descendants had already migrated across the Bering Land Bridge and survived in Eurasia. From this perspective, the horse did not *arrive* here five centuries ago, it *returned*— and the people were ready for it.

However you want to explain it, throughout the 1700s America's quintessential Song of the Open Road would have been an exuberant, high-pitched Indian chant, exclaimed full-throated from the back of a galloping horse, punctuated by the thunder of hooves, and reverberating off the blue-vision hills that suddenly were not so far away.

The road song of the next century had a different melody. In 1803, one hundred years before Horatio Nelson Jackson set off from San Francisco hoping to become the first American to drive an automobile across the continent, Meriwether Lewis departed Washington, D.C., looking to become the first American to cross the continent, period. (He picked up William Clark in Louisville and other members of the Corps of Discovery along the way, so despite the immense contributions of these others to the expedition's overall success, Lewis was the only one eligible for the coast-to-coast laurels.) Traveling by keelboat and canoe, horseback and on foot, it took him nearly two and a half years to make it from the Atlantic to the Pacific.

One way to summarize nineteenth-century American history, in the aftermath of Lewis and Clark, is a nation in a perpetual rush to find better and faster ways to reach the next horizon . . . and the next, and the next, until the country's vast

A restless nation moves westward. ➤

but alluring distances were conquered. All those horizons, so little time.

Beginning in the 1840s, the quest for gold, for land, or the chance to start over sent hundreds of thousands of pioneers to Oregon and California—restless Americans like William Swain, a farmer from upstate New York, who kissed his wife and baby goodbye, took a series of canal boats and river steamers to Independence, Missouri, and then joined a wagon train bound for the gold fields. Seven grueling months after leaving his family, when he straggled at last into California, he immediately wrote back to his brother, saying, "For God's sake . . . stay at home." But despite having failed utterly as a prospector, as an old and successful orchardist back in New York the story he most loved to tell his grandchildren was of his journey across the country in the Days of '49.

Later travelers rode the overland stagecoach, which cut the time in half. Mark Twain was one of them, going from Missouri to Nevada in 1861 with his piously serious brother to escape the carnage of the Civil War. Riding on the coach's roof, clothed only in his underwear, he reveled in the scenery as the stage rattled through the western mountains: "Ham and eggs and scenery, a 'down-grade,' a flying coach, a fragrant pipe and a contented heart—these make happiness. It is what all the ages have struggled for." But by the time he reached the end of the Nevada deserts, Twain had concluded that stage travel was so bumpy and dusty that he was glad his brother had brought along an unabridged dictionary, "because we never could have found language to tell how glad we were, in any sort of dictionary but an unabridged one with pictures in it."

By 1869, the first transcontinental railroad was completed, and Americans could now cross their nation in a matter of weeks instead of months or years—provided they were content to confine themselves to a railroad schedule. The remainder of the century was pretty much consumed by extending the railroad's reach to nearly every recess of the country. Not coincidentally, these years also marked the final military conquest of native peoples, in particular the last holdouts, the horse nomads of the Great Plains, who found themselves confined to reservations roughly a century and a half after they had first galloped onto the prairies and felt the wind rush into their lungs.

As the last Indian horse herds were being turned in (or destroyed by the Army), a strange—and revealing—thing occurred in the popular imagination. The feathered warrior on horseback had become a national image of all Indians and of noble freedom—even though the culture it represented had just been subjugated, even though most tribes had never been nomadic horsemen, even though their moment of glory had been so historically brief. The same thing would soon happen to cowboys.

Late in the nineteenth century, the Iron Horse ruled the range. But despite its undisputed power and dominance, and perhaps because it seemed so impersonal, so industrial, so constrained by two steel rails to travel only in a straight line, it could never compete with the image of a lone horseman (Indian or cowboy) to communicate unfettered freedom. It would take something entirely new to do that—something that combined a bit of the locomotive's power with some of the mobility of a horse. And once again, while it would appear in Europe first, America is where it would become the icon of a culture utterly transformed by it. At the dawn of the twentieth century, the Song of the Open Road was about to be punctuated by a car horn and the clatter of an internal combustion engine.

The earth expanding right hand and left hand,
The picture alive, every part in its best light,
The music falling in where it is wanted, and stopping
*   where it is not wanted,*
The cheerful voice of the public road—the gay fresh
*   sentiment of the road.*

I think whatever I shall meet on the road I shall like,
*   and whoever beholds me shall like me;*
I think whoever I see must be happy.

I imagine that the first few days of Horatio Nelson Jackson's trip were the most exhilarating: The departure from San Francisco on that May afternoon of 1903, the salt breeze on the Oakland ferry, then hitting that first country road and opening up the *Vermont*, climbing to ten, fifteen, then twenty miles per hour, maybe even pushing it to the limits of thirty mph or more, just to test it—and himself—out. ("A horseman driving a spirited equine will go fast or slow as he releases or increases the pressure upon the sensitive mouth through the driving reins," the Winton Company's sale brochure explained, extolling its revolutionary precursor to a gas pedal. "With the Winton control the motor speeds up and the car forges ahead when the foot button pressure is increased. Speed of car diminishes when the pressure is released. . . . One quickly learns to operate the governor foot button by instinct.") Watching the miles click by on the cyclometer. Adjusting the goggles to protect his eyes from the clouds of dust his whirling tires were creating. Attuning his ears to the nuances of noise pouring out of the two-cylinder engine directly beneath his seat. Getting to know the feel of the vehicle while handling curves, hills, bumps, and stops. Even the first blowout on the first day was probably more exciting—*Pffffffffft! Watch out!*—than it was exasperating, since they still made eighty-three miles that afternoon and Jackson was blessedly insulated from the foreknowledge of how many tire problems and delays awaited him down the road.

That's the way it is with all road trips—and anyone who has spent any time crossing the nation in an automobile immediately recognizes in Jackson's journey the template for all the American road trips that followed. In the early part, with anticipation pumping the adrenaline, everything is fresh and new, and all horizons brim with promise. In the case of Jackson's psychic engine, multiply that a hundredfold. As his letters to his wife (and peripatetic career after his journey) so clearly attest, his innate energy and optimism ran on high octane to begin with. Add to the mix just how *new* the whole experience really was for Jackson—not just the unfamiliar scenery, but the viscerally new experience of the way he was traversing it. With no windshield and no top on the *Vermont*, he met the landscape head-on, seeing it, smelling it, feeling it unfold before him, so unlike the side-view-only perspective from the window of a closed railroad car. And unlike a horse-and-wagon, his car propelled him down the road at both greater speed and for longer, sustained stretches of time. (Eighty-three miles in an afternoon—including a stop to change a tire—was not a typical outing for a horse-and-buggy.) Now add in Jackson's knowledge that what he was doing was not only new for him personally, but new in his people's experience, and the word "exhilaration" suddenly seems somewhat inadequate.

He must have felt like the first Cheyenne who grabbed the mane of a Spanish pony, swung himself up on its back, kicked its flank, and found himself hurtling across the endless grasslands. For Jackson, the "blue vision" was even more distant, an entire continent away, but particularly in the early rush of the journey, he could see it clearly and it probably seemed within easy reach.

Then came the inevitable troubles and annoyances of the road: More blown tires. Running out of gas, then oil. Delays for parts, delays for repairs. Belongings lost or forgotten along the way. Nights interrupted by snoring strangers or bug-ridden beds. The price-gouging merchant. The inedible meal. Bad weather and worse roads. Getting lost and facing the almost unbearable prospect of having to retrace your day's route. (As a historical note, it's worth mentioning that Jackson, like Lewis and Clark before him, had absolutely no compunctions about stopping to ask directions, proving, I think,

Dust and scenery on the overland stage ➤

that American males must have developed their obsession against it sometime later. Although it's probably also worth observing that no Indians ever deliberately pointed the Corps of Discovery in the wrong direction, simply to give some relatives the chance to see their first white man; maybe Jackson's experience with the girl on the white horse marked a cultural turning point.)

He met it all with remarkably unflappable good humor. If "we proceeded on" became the most recurrent phrase in the Lewis and Clark journals, "the worst of it is over" keeps jumping out of Jackson's letters to his wife (usually just before something even worse happens to his plans). One phrase is filled with a kind of grim determination; the other is evidence of either boundless confidence or Pollyannaism bordering on delusion. I prefer to think of Jackson on the confident side of that equation, and as a longtime student of the road have concluded that "the worst of it is over" pairs nicely with "we proceeded on" as the proper attitude for crossing the continent and accomplishing something no one else ever has.

Following his trail, there were many times I wished Jackson had spent more time recording his experience. Take the sagebrush country, for instance. Traveling ten to twenty miles per hour may have seemed fast to his generation, but it still doesn't get you across great distances very quickly. For thirty-two days, more than half his time on the road, in the vast space from Alturas, California, to somewhere east of Rawlins, Wyoming, Jackson would have been traveling through one kind of sage or another virtually every day. A month of sagebrush at a speed lower than a school zone's. In that same time, Meriwether Lewis would have produced lengthy descriptions of every variation of sagebrush he encountered, tested its taste and possible medicinal uses, compared it to buffalo dung and cottonwood as a fuel source, elicited local customs and beliefs associated with it, attempted at least one lyrical passage featuring it ("*This morning the sun's glancing rays off the blue and green sagebrush presented a most romantic appearance. . . .*"), and probably thrown in numerous other journal entries about how everyone on the expedition felt about it ("*Men complain much about the sage, which they say seems to have no end. . . .*" or "*My dog seems constantly bothered by the brush obstructing his view. . . .*"). Mark Twain was more succinct—and colorful. "Sage-brush," he wrote from Nevada, "is very fair fuel, but as a vegetable it is a distinguished failure. . . . When crushed, sage-brush emits an odor which isn't exactly magnolia and equally isn't exactly polecat—but it is a sort of compromise between the two."

Jackson, by contrast, mentions the sage only four times by my count, and always briefly—twice saying that bad roads forced him and Sewall Crocker to steer the *Vermont* through the open sage (in one instance stripping off the cyclometer), and twice offering merely that they cut some sagebrush to place under the car's wheels in hopes of getting out of a mud hole. It would be patently unfair to hold Jackson up to the standards of Twain and Lewis, two of America's greatest travel correspondents, but I might have at least expected him to comment on the startlingly fragrant aroma (more magnolia than polecat) that uncrushed sagebrush emits after a rainstorm, since he experienced both in such abundance.

I also would have appreciated more descriptions of the scenery from his perspective, more details of the trip beyond Omaha (when he became so intent on reaching New York that his letter-writing essentially stopped), more elaboration on the personality of his faithful traveling assistant, Sewall Crocker, beyond the statement "He is a mighty good man." (And I often wished that Crocker—the William Clark to Jackson's Meriwether Lewis—had given us his own impressions of the journey.) I would have liked a little more about the dog, Bud. (Did he bark at every farm animal they passed? Where did he sleep at night? Was he more companion than guard dog?) But those are minor quibbles com-

pared to the prospect that Jackson might have left behind no on-the-spot written record at all. "Please keep my letters as I want them for reference," he instructed his wife in his very first letter, a day after leaving San Francisco. We're lucky that she did.

The essence of his character radiates from those letters. A vibrant yet tender love for his wife is in all of them—from the breezy, playful salutations toward "Swipes" and "you dear little girl" to his recurring apologies for the prolonged separation his quirky yet historic odyssey was causing; from his sweet effort to surprise her with an anniversary dress ordered from the wilds of Wyoming to the urgency ("Watch me now come to you") of his desire to be in her presence once more. His "worst of it is over" spirit exudes from every page. There are elements of confidence as well as irrepressible energy in that spirit, and a likable individualism (evident, for instance, when he turns down the Winton Company's offer to subsidize and organize the last half of his expedition).

But what emerges most clearly is just how thoroughly he was enjoying his adventure, despite mudholes and misdirections, broken parts and rocky trails, choking dust and long days without the prospect of a comfortable bed or a warm meal. Teddy Roosevelt, touring the West by train that same summer, no doubt would have pronounced it "bully" to spend

a few days with Jackson splashing across streams or rattling up mountainsides in the *Vermont;* the worse the weather, the bullier; the more physical the exertion required to dig out of buffalo wallows or push boulders out of the way, the bullier yet.

What also emerges from the letters is how much Jackson (just like Roosevelt) loved creating a sensation—not just at the end of his trip, when he was entering the history books, but perhaps even more so near the beginning, on those rough trails and in those remote towns where people who had never seen an automobile in motion dove for cover under their wagons as the *Vermont* approached, where crowds alerted by excited telegraph messages would line the street for hours, fully expecting that the first horseless carriage to enter their village might zoom through at ninety miles an hour, where schools let out because seeing a "real live auto" seemed more important than the day's lessons (just as later children would watch televisions in their classrooms to see a moon landing), where sharp-eyed farmers and ranchers would curiously inspect the *Vermont* and then offer something in trade for the chance to ride in it, and where sweat-stained blacksmiths, as they assisted Crocker in making some repairs, surely began thinking seriously about expanding their line of services.

If, in the early 1700s, some Cheyenne traditionalists argued that the young men parading by on horseback were indulging in a passing fancy or clung to the belief that the time-honored dog culture would never disappear, oral histories have blessedly spared them from embarrassment by erasing them from memory. More than likely, however, such skeptics existed. Two centuries later, Jackson crossed the West during a similar moment in time, when doubts about the automobile's future were not only widespread but well-documented. But as he and the *Vermont* passed through each town, and then as news of his progress began to spread throughout the nation—*A car, all the way across the continent!*—you can almost feel the direction of America's cultural history turning, because the compass arrow of our restlessness had found a new magnetic pole.

At the start of the nineteenth century, Lewis and Clark had crossed the continent and pointed that restlessness westward. The nation followed and was changed forever. Jackson's trip at the start of the twentieth century, admittedly not nearly as epic or far-reaching as the Corps of Discovery's, nevertheless heralded that another new era of dramatic change, for good and for ill, was beginning—one in which Americans would satisfy their restless yearnings by giving themselves outright to the automobile.

◄ *The iron horse: more speed, less freedom*

The more I studied Jackson's journey and retraced his route, the more I realized that while he had set the pattern for every subsequent American automobile road trip, he had also been connecting into something much deeper in our national experience, something that had nothing to do with the gasoline internal combustion engine.

I don't know whether sometime in the near future the automobile will go the way of the horse-and-wagon (although my teenage daughter, Emmy, who for at least three years has been counting down the days until she turns sixteen and can get her driver's license, has pretty much convinced me that the American equation of "automobile equals freedom" still has some life left in it after a hundred years). I do know what I've learned about the cycles of history from the road—and the road teaches such lessons well, since it keeps bumping into history at every intersection.

The Song of the Open Road, sung now for centuries on this continent, has many different verses. It has been reinterpreted by each succeeding generation, sometimes set to a new beat and accompanied by new instruments, but they are mostly variations on the same theme. It's not the getting there that matters so much as the *going*. If it's happiness we think we're after, it's the *pursuit* that actually makes us happy. Somehow, the song seems born within each of us.

And for some reason, consciously or not, it's a tune that we pass along.

To know the universe itself as a road—as many roads—
as roads for traveling souls.

The Soul travels;
The body does not travel as much as the soul;
The body has just as great a work as the soul, and parts
away at last for the journeys of the soul.

Faced with the need a year ago to travel from our home in New Hampshire to the state of Iowa, my son, Will, and I decided to turn it into what we call a "buddy trip." In his twelve years, we've taken a number of such journeys. Once, when he was seven, we drove to Rhode Island and back, simply so he could check it off from the ever-dwindling list of states he's never visited. When he was eight, we decided to take a looping route that allowed him to pick a stone from the shore of each Great Lake (and as a bonus, see Niagara Falls). His ninth summer, he and I broke away from a family vacation in the West to scout along Horatio Nelson Jackson's route in northwestern California and southeastern Oregon, covering in one day a section Jackson took more than a week to cross.

For the buddy trip to Iowa, Will's principal goal was to eliminate Ohio, Indiana, Kentucky, and Tennessee from his To Do list. My motivation was different. We were going back to my hometown for my father's funeral (my wife, Dianne, and Emmy would be flying there to join us), and I thought I needed something to take my mind off the real purpose of the trip—although once we were under way, especially on those early mornings when I roused my son from sleep to get a quick

Dudley and Dayton Duncan, 1959

start on the day, just as my own dad used to wake me in the predawn darkness for long drives to go pheasant hunting or fishing, I realized that perhaps what I really was seeking was reconnecting with his memory before saying goodbye to his remains.

Driving along, more memories enveloped me. I remembered how I once sat in the backseat as a young boy, study-

ing how my dad handled the steering wheel, left arm resting on the open window ledge; remembered trips to the Black Hills and the headwaters of the Mississippi; remembered him in the passenger seat, me behind the wheel at last, nervously easing our car into the passing lane for the first time under his guidance. And I remembered taking him out in his car shortly before his death, to drive him around the county that had been his home for eighty-one years.

Both of us knew without saying that this would be his last car ride. We cruised the streets of town as he pointed out places where the milestones of his life took place. We took gravel roads and a state highway to see the farm where my mother had grown up, and he talked of their romantic road trip to Kansas City in 1942 to elope. We even drove out to the interstate for a short spin, because he was curi-

162 ous to see how his fifteen-year-old car would hold up at turnpike speeds.

"Black care," Teddy Roosevelt once wrote, "rarely sits behind a rider whose pace is fast enough." There's something about the open road that promises new beginnings as it simultaneously peels back layer upon layer of the past. Out on the farthest horizon, all lines converge.

On a map, the route Will and I ended up taking to Iowa looks as if we wanted to

Dayton and Will Duncan, 2003

avoid ever getting there. We spent the first night in Gettysburg, Pennsylvania, and used up the next morning touring the battlefield before another long drive brought us to Charleston, West Virginia. With an earlier departure the next day, we had breakfast (one of the worst biscuits-and-gravy imaginable) in Ohio, ate lunch (a delicious cheeseburger at a hole-in-the-wall called Bob's) in Indiana, toured Mammoth Cave National Park in Kentucky, and reached

Nashville, Tennessee, in time for supper at a place that serves Southern food with iced tea in a Mason jar. We washed the miles off with a late-night dip in the motel pool, and Will went to bed content in the knowledge that four more states were under his belt.

Before reaching Iowa three days later, he had tasted his first grits (and loved them); we had spotted license plates from forty-eight states (all but North Dakota and Hawaii); our maroonish Suburban had been officially named *Redbud* in honor of the beautiful flowering trees lining the roads (winning out over my initial suggestion of *Old Rusty*); I had become as conversant as Will in the song lyrics of Weird Al Yankovic (while he had joined me in the ranks of Marty Robbins experts); and raccoons had taken the lead over opossums in the informal roadkill count we were keeping. We had stopped to watch the mighty Ohio empty into the even mightier Mississippi. We had toured the excavation of an ancient Indian mound village in Illinois. We had inspected a life-sized replica of Lewis and Clark's keelboat in St. Charles, Missouri. We had visited Mark Twain's birthplace and his boyhood home in Hannibal, then explored the limestone cave he made famous in *The Adventures of Tom Sawyer.*

By the time we pulled into Indianola, a small town south of Des Moines, we had added several chapters to our own book of adventures. Like Horatio Nelson Jackson, we had seen the country, touched its history, created imperishable memories. We, ourselves, were good fortune. Strong and content, we had traveled the open road.

Allons! the road is before us!
It is safe—I have tried it—my own feet have tried
it well.

Will you give me yourself? will you come travel
with me?
Shall we stick by each other as long as we live?

DATE	ITINERARY
May 23	San Francisco to Tracy, California
May 24	To Sacramento, California
May 25	To Oroville, California
May 26	To Anderson, California
May 27	To Montgomery, California
May 28	To Bieber, California
May 29	To Alturas, California
May 30	Delayed in Alturas
May 31	Delayed in Alturas
June 1	Delayed in Alturas
June 2	To Lakeview, Oregon
June 3	Delayed in Lakeview
June 4	Delayed in Lakeview
June 5	Delayed in Lakeview
June 6	To SL Ranch, Oregon
June 7	To Silver Creek, Oregon
June 8	To Burns, Oregon
June 9	To Vale, Oregon
June 10	To Ontario, Oregon
June 11	To Caldwell, Idaho
June 12	To Orchard, Idaho
June 13	To somewhere east of Mountain Home, Idaho
June 14	Stuck somewhere east of Hailey, Idaho
June 15	To Pocatello, Idaho
June 16	To Soda Springs, Idaho
June 17	To Montpelier, Idaho
June 18	To Diamondville, Wyoming
June 19	Stuck somewhere near Opal, Wyoming
June 20	Lost near the Green River
June 21	To Rock Springs, Wyoming
June 22	Stuck west of Bitter Creek, Wyoming
June 23	To Rawlins, Wyoming
June 24	Delayed in Rawlins
June 25	Delayed in Rawlins
June 26	Delayed in Rawlins
June 27	Delayed in Rawlins
June 28	Delayed in Rawlins
June 29	To somewhere west of Laramie, Wyoming
June 30	To Laramie, Wyoming
July 1	To Cheyenne, Wyoming
July 2	To Archer, Wyoming
July 3	Delayed in Archer
July 4	Delayed in Archer
July 5	Delayed in Archer
July 6	Delayed in Archer
July 7	Toward Nebraska
July 8	Through Julesburg, Colorado, and Ogallala, Nebraska
July 9	Through North Platte, Nebraska
July 10	Somewhere in central Nebraska
July 11	Through Kearney and Columbus, Nebraska
July 12	To Omaha, Nebraska
July 13	Through western Iowa
July 14	Through Marshalltown, Iowa
July 15	Through Clinton, Iowa
July 16	Through Dixon, Illinois
July 17	To Chicago
July 18	To South Bend, Indiana
July 19	To Toledo, Ohio
July 20	To Cleveland
July 21	To Buffalo, New York
July 22	To somewhere west of Rochester, New York
July 23	To Syracuse, New York
July 24	To Little Falls, New York
July 25	En route to New York City without overnight
July 26	Arrive New York City

Our first and most profound thanks go to Mary Louise Blanchard and Ann Wall, granddaughters of Horatio Nelson Jackson, who generously permitted us access to his unpublished letters and private photographs; and to Dianne Kearns Duncan, whose untiring detective work connected us to them. While we had been moving forward on this project before we knew of Ann and Mary Louise and their collection of letters, in retrospect we can't imagine making our film or completing this book without them. Our hope is that we have now told Jackson's story and brought his irrepressible American spirit to life in a way that makes his granddaughters as proud of the storytelling as they rightfully are of their grandfather and his achievement.

A more complete list of the film credits appears elsewhere, but we want to give special thanks to Tom Hanks for agreeing to be the voice of Horatio Nelson Jackson and bringing his great talent to the task; to Keith David, for reading the narration with the perfect combination of authority and whimsy; to Allen Moore, who retraced Jackson's route with us, vividly capturing the adventure and the scenery on film; and to Erik Ewers, who edited the film with such artistry, assisted by Craig Mellish.

For both the book and the film, we particularly would like to single out Susanna Steisel, Pam Tubridy Baucom, and Jennifer Stanelle, whose dedication and discerning eyes discovered so many compelling photographic images from Jackson's era. As always, the entire Florentine Films family was involved in this project in one way or another, wearing many hats and making sure that what some people call work, we call a pleasure and a privilege: Paul Barnes, Brenda Heath, Patty Lawlor, Sean Huff, Lynn Novick, Geoffrey C. Ward, Sarah Botstein, Erin Lester, Elle Carriére, Roger Haydock, Bobby Horton, Jacqueline Schwab—and the late Meg Anne Schindler, who brought so much joy to all of us.

Our film could not have been made without the financial support of General Motors and our other sponsors: the Arthur Vining Davis Foundations, the Park Foundation, the Corporation for Public Broadcasting, and the Public Broadcasting System. We also wish to thank our friends at WETA in Washington; our agents Gerry McCauley and Chuck Verrill; our editor, Ashbel Green; and this book's designer, Wendy Byrne.

Finally, we thank our families—Sarah and Lilly Burns, and Dianne, Emmy, and Will Duncan. They put up with our absences when the road calls us away, and then put up with us again when they find themselves traveling with two guys who refuse to stop for directions and who always want to add just a few more miles before the sun goes down.

Ken Burns
Dayton Duncan
Walpole, New Hampshire

Most of the first-person accounts of Horatio Nelson Jackson—and many of the details about his historic trip—used in this book are drawn from the previously unpublished letters and telegrams he dispatched from the road to his wife, Bertha. These on-the-road commentaries not only provide fresh insights into Jackson's character but illuminate innumerable details that heretofore were great blanks in the story. The letters and telegrams belong to the Jacksons' granddaughters, Mary Louise Blanchard and Ann Wall, who graciously granted us permission for their use. Numbering forty-five in total, they begin on May 24, 1903, when Jackson had reached Sacramento on his second day out, and conclude on July 23, with a short telegram from Rochester, New York, a few days before the completion of his journey. If Jackson kept a cursory journal or trip log (as indicated in at least one newspaper account from New York City), it has not been found. Similarly, the letters Bertha sent to her "wandering boy" from home, which he mentions receiving at several stops along the way, have not surfaced.

Three other first-person accounts exist: a letter Jackson wrote to the Winton Motor Carriage Company on July 29, 1903, recounting his adventure (published immediately in the company's monthly, *The Auto Era*, vol. II, nos. 11–12); a retrospective account he penned in 1936 for *The American Legion Monthly* (and later republished in the Burlington *Daily News* as "It's History Now" on June 26,

1944, in conjunction with the donation of Jackson's car to the Smithsonian Institution); and "I Made the First Cross-Country Auto Trip," as told to William Engle, *The American Weekly*, May 17, 1953. In a few instances, we have combined those accounts with his letters.

Two previous books have dealt with Jackson's trip. *The Mad Doctor's Drive* by Ralph Nading Hill (Stephen Greene Press, 1964) is a short, rollicking account of the trip's highlights, gleaned partly from an interview Hill conducted with Jackson fifty years after the fact. (It has recently been republished—along with a Winton sales brochure and instruction manual from 1903—by the Peter C. Kesling Foundation in LaPorte, Indiana.) *Coast to Coast by Automobile: The Pioneering Trips, 1899–1908* by Curt McConnell (Stanford University Press, 2000) devotes a chapter to Jackson's trip—as well as chapters dealing with the aborted attempts by the Davises and Alexander Winton, the successful Packard and Oldsmobile expeditions of 1903, and a number of subsequent cross-country road trips.

In addition to those sources and the many newspaper accounts quoted in this book, other principal sources include:

Finch, Christopher. *Highways to Heaven: The AUTO Biography of America*. New York, 1992.

Hokanson, Drake. *The Lincoln Highway: Main Street Across America*. Iowa City, 1989.

Mahoney, Tom. "First Car Across the U.S.A." *Mechanix Illustrated*. March 1953.

Sears, Stephen W. "Ocean to Ocean in an Automobile Car." *American Heritage*. June/July, 1980.

Sheridan, Martin. "Colonel Nelson Jackson: The Man Who Spent $8,000 to Win a $50 Bet." *Finance*. September 15, 1951.

———. "The First Car Across the U.S." *Yankee*. February 1952.

———. "The First Automobile Coast to Coast." *True's Yearbook*. June 1952.

Vaughan, David K. "First Automobile to Cross the United States." *Strut & Axle*. Vol. VII, No. 4, 1985.

Wilson, Paul C. *Chrome Dream*. Radnor, Pa.

Winton Motor Carriage Co. "Across the Continent in a Winton." *Ocean to Ocean in a Winton*. 1903.

Wolf, Thomas H. "The Object at Hand." *Smithsonian*. October 1990.

ILLUSTRATION CREDITS

ARCHIVE ABBREVIATIONS
JHU: Johns Hopkins University, Milton S. Eisenhower Library
NAHC: National Automotive History Collection, Detroit Public Library
MLB: Mary Louise Blanchard
UVM: University of Vermont, Special Collections

ENDPAPERS
MapQuest.com

FRONTISPIECE
i: UVM ii–iii: UVM

PREFACE: THE WAY WE ENTER OUR HISTORY
vi: Walpole Historical Society, F2-30 viii: Craig Mellish xi: Craig Mellish xii: Craig Mellish 1: Walpole Historical Society, F2-32

ONE: A PASSING MECHANICAL FANCY
2–3: UVM 4: Oakland Museum of California, A79.39.10 5: San Francisco University Club 6–7: Milwaukee Public Museum, 43582 6: Minnesota Historical Society, 409, HE3.1/p100 7: (**left**) Hulton/Archive by Getty Images, JF1564; (**right**) Brown Brothers 8–9: Library of Congress, LC-D4 1929 8: NAHC 9: (**left**) Brown Brothers; (**right**) Oldsmobile History Center, 89-325, drawer 1A-1900 and earlier,

Folder 12217 **10–11**: Stanford University, Green Library, Hart Stereo, 356 **10**: Seaver Center for Western History Research, Los Angeles County Museum of Natural History, #6843 **11**: Jerry Grulkey **12**: JHU, Levy Collection, Box: 060, Item: 066 **13**: Culver Pictures, PHT 003 SS001 002 **14**: Brown Brothers **15**: University of Rochester Library, D-251, 3:19 **16**: *Cleveland Plain Dealer*, May 21, 1901 **17**: *Auto Era*, November 1901 **18**: MLB **19**: MLB **20**: Marilyn Vogt **21**: (**left**) UVM; (**right**) UVM **22–23**: UVM

TWO: THE HARDEST WORK I EVER DID
24–25: UVM 26: Minnesota Historical Society, HF4.7/P3 Negative#26003 27: MLB 28–29: Culver Pictures, Auto 27 CP001 073 28: Eric Merklein 30: Osher Library, University of Southern Maine 31: UVM 33: UVM 34: (**left**) UVM; (**right**) UVM 36: UVM 37: UVM

THREE: ONE OF THE WONDERS OF THE CENTURY
38–39: Modoc County Historical Museum, 1172-C 40: Modoc County Historical Museum, P-1202 41: MLB 42: Schminck Memorial Museum 43: (inset) *Lakeview Herald,* June 4, 1903, Smithsonian Institution 43: Lake County District Library 44: Harney County Historical Society 45: UVM

46: UVM 47: UVM 48–49: UVM 48: UVM 51: UVM 52: Harney County Historical Society

FOUR: AN ENTHUSIAST FOR MOTORING
54–55: UVM 56: Community Library, Ketchum, Idaho, F00536 57: MLB 58–59: Iowa Department of Transportation Archives 58: NAHC 59: *The Auto Era*, March 1903, courtesy of Marilyn Vogt 60–61: Minnesota Historical Society, HE3.8/r36 60: NAHC, Roads: Oldsmobile 1902 63: Grant Lau 64–65: UVM 66: UVM 67: UVM 69: *Saturday Evening Post,* 1903 70–71: NAHC, *Worlds Work,* May 1904 72: NAHC 73: NAHC

FIVE: THE WORST OF IT IS OVER
74–75: UVM 76: UVM 77: UVM 78: UVM 79: Carbon County Museum 81: Carbon County Museum 82–83: Wyoming State Archives, J. E. Stimson Collection 84: UVM 85: MLB 86: Wyoming State Archives, J. E. Stimson Collection 87: UVM 89: John Hammond 90: *Saturday Evening Post,* 1903, courtesy of Dartmouth College Library 90–91: Oldsmobile History Center, Lansing, Michigan

SIX: BUFFALO WALLOWS
92–93: UVM 94: UVM 95: *Omaha*

Morning World Herald, July 13, 1903, Smithsonian Institution 96–97: Culver Pictures, ROA003 CP001 021 97: Culver Pictures, AUT015 CP001 020 98: MLB 99: UVM 100: UVM 103: Western Reserve Historical Society, 1903 Winton Morgue File 104: UVM 105: MLB 106: NAHC 107: *The Automobile,* July 25, 1903, NAHC 108–109: NAHC 108: *The Automobile,* Aug. 15, 1903 109: NAHC 110: Oldsmobile History Center, Lansing, Michigan 111: *Motor Age,* August 13, 1903

SEVEN: WATCH ME NOW
112–113: Rochester Public Library, rpf 00935 114: University of Rochester Library, D-251, 7:1 115: UVM 116: Brown Brothers 117: George Eastman House, 5.2 14446 118–119: NAHC 120–121: NAHC 120: *New-York Daily Tribune,* July 30, 1903 121: *The World,* July 27, 1903 122–123: Walpole Historical Society, F2-34 123: (**left**) *The Auto Era*, July–August 1903; (**right**) *The Auto Era*, September 1903 125: NAHC 126: Free Library of Philadelphia 127: Library of Congress, LC-D4-50036

EIGHT: A SIGNAL TRIUMPH
128–129: Denver Public Library: Western History Collection, P1905

130: Culver Pictures, AUT015 CP001 099 **131:** Culver Pictures, SGN001 CP001 041 **133:** NAHC **134–135:** NAHC **134: (top left)** JHU, Levy Collection, Box: 060, Item: 056; **(top right)** JHU, Levy Collection, Box: 060, Item: 062; **(center)** JHU, Levy Collection, Box: 060, Item: 157; **(bottom left)** JHU, Levy Collection, Box: 060, Item: 016; **(bottom right)** JHU, Levy Collection, Box: 060, Item: 088 **136–137:** Culver Pictures, ROA005 CP001 033 **136:** Nebraska Historical Society, RG 2608-2387 **137: (left)** Nebraska Historical Society, RG 2608-2849; **(right)** Culver Pictures, ROA005 CP001 024 **138–139:** Culver Pictures, ROA003 CP001 024 **140:** MLB **141:** UVM **142–143:** University of Michigan, lhc 0325

AFTERWORD: SONG OF THE OPEN ROAD

144: University of Michigan, lhc 1101 **147:** University of Michigan, lhc 1240 **148:** Dartmouth College Library, E. S. Curtis Collection **151:** Denver Public Library: Western History Collection, F20883 **155:** Idaho State Historical Society, 73.221.55/B **158:** Library of Congress, LC Z62 63447 **161:** Dayton Duncan **162:** Daniel J. White

BACKMATTER

164: Florentine Films/MapQuest.com **166:** UVM **169:** UVM **175:** UVM

In Loving Memory of
ROBERT K. BURNS, Jr.
DUDLEY DUNCAN
MEG ANNE SCHINDLER

———

A FILM DIRECTED BY
KEN BURNS

WRITTEN BY
DAYTON DUNCAN

PRODUCED BY
DAYTON DUNCAN
&
KEN BURNS

EDITED BY
ERIK EWERS

CINEMATOGRAPHY
ALLEN MOORE
KEN BURNS

"HORATIO CAM" DIGITAL FOOTAGE
ALLEN MOORE

ASSOCIATE PRODUCER
SUSANNA STEISEL

COORDINATING PRODUCER
PAM TUBRIDY BAUCOM

FIELD PRODUCER
CRAIG MELLISH

NARRATED BY
KEITH DAVID

THE VOICE OF HORATIO NELSON JACKSON
TOM HANKS

OTHER VOICES
ADAM ARKIN
TOM BODETT
PHILIP BOSCO
KEVIN CONWAY
JOHN CULLUM
MURPHY GUYER
AMY MADIGAN
GEORGE PLIMPTON
ELI WALLACH

ASSISTANT EDITOR
CRAIG MELLISH

PROGRAM ADVISERS
ROGER ALLISON
PAUL BARNES
TIM CLARK
JULIE DUNFEY
DRAKE HOKANSON
PETER KESLING
CURT McCONNELL
LYNN NOVICK
GEOFFREY C. WARD

CHIEF FINANCIAL OFFICER
BRENDA HEATH

ASSOCIATE FINANCIAL OFFICER
PATTY LAWLOR

ADMINISTRATIVE ASSISTANTS
ERIN LESTER
MEG ANNE SCHINDLER
TESS DEDDO
ELLE CARRIERE

ASSISTANT ASSOCIATE PRODUCER
JENNIFER STANELLE

TECHNICAL DIRECTOR
SEAN HUFF

SOUND EDITORS
SEAN HUFF
ERIK EWERS
CRAIG MELLISH

MUSIC EDITOR
CRAIG MELLISH

SOUND POST-PRODUCTION
SOUND ONE

RE-RECORDING MIXER
LEE DICHTER
MARTIN CZEMBOR

ASSISTANT CAMERA
ROGER HAYDOCK

ANIMATION STAND PHOTOGRAPHY
THE FRAME SHOP
Edward Joyce and Edward Searles

STILL PHOTOGRAPHY
STEPHEN PETEGORSKY

VOICE-OVER RECORDING
Lou Verrico
FULL HOUSE PRODUCTIONS

OTHER VOICE-OVER RECORDING
WAVES, Hollywood, CA
Bobby Garza

SOUND RECORDING
JOHN OSBORNE
STEVEN GOTTLIEB
SEAN HUFF
MORGAN WESSON

RESEARCH ASSISTANTS
DIANNE KEARNS DUNCAN
MIKE HILL
MELISSA KLEIN
JOSH BROWN
BETH MAGURA
DEBRA KELLER
RANDY MILLER
BETHANY POWELL
BRIAN FERGUSON-AVERY
JANE McLEAN
KIMBERLY HAMLIN

POST-PRODUCTION ASSISTANT
DAN WHITE

POST-PRODUCTION INTERNS
TYLER COTE
MELANIE CUNNINGHAM
TESS DEDDO
IAN DENNY
HEATHER DURFEY
IAN ESCHELMAN
RYAN GIFFORD
KATHERINE HAAS
ANDREW HAGENBUCH
ZACHARY MAYNARD
KRYSTYNA MORT
BETHANY POWELL
BRIAN PUTNAM
LIZ SERU
ANGELA SNOW
TEO ZAGAR

NEGATIVE MATCHING
NOELLE PENRAAT

TITLE DESIGN
JAMES MADDEN

MAPS
MAPQUEST.COM
Creative Mapping Solutions
Mountville, PA

COLOR
DUART FILM LABS

SPIRIT DATA CINE FILM TRANSFER
THE TAPE HOUSE
John J. Dowdell III

ON-LINE EDITING
THE TAPE HOUSE

DIGITAL IMAGING
STEPHEN PETEGORSKY
ANDREW HAGENBUCH
DAN WHITE

LEGAL SERVICES
ROBERT N. GOLD

INSTRUMENTALIST AND STUDIO ARRANGEMENTS
BOBBY HORTON

TRADITIONAL MUSIC
JACQUELINE SCHWAB, piano

MUSIC RECORDED AT
SOUNDESIGN
Brattleboro, Vermont

MUSIC ENGINEERS
BILLY SHAW
ALAN STOCKWELL

LOCATIONS
The University Club, San Francisco
Urritia Ranch

STOCK FOOTAGE
Historical Films
Imagebank by Getty Images
John E. Allen

EXTRA SPECIAL THANKS
MARY LOUISE BLANCHARD
ANN WALL
DIANNE KEARNS DUNCAN

SPECIAL THANKS
The People of Walpole,
New Hampshire
Antique Wireless Association
L. A. Burdick Chocolates
Com Three Marketing
Dartmouth College Libraries
Greater Falls Travel
HB Communications, Inc.
Historical Society of
Cheshire County
Mason Library, Keene State College
The Park Hyatt, Washington, DC
Smithsonian Institution
Walpole Historical Society

Roger Allison
Anne Ames
Dennis Bolen
Sarah Botstein
Carol Butler
Bernie Golias
Jan Grenci
Jerry Grulkey
John Hammond
Peg Holmes

Larry and Donna Hughes
Becky Jones
Bonnie Jones
Steve Lubar
Jeffrey Marshall
Curt McConnell
Carolyn McCormick
Eric Merklein
Lois Merry
William Mintzer
Allen Ruben
Mike Sturgeon
Roger B. White
Jim Winton
Marilyn Winton Vogt

———————

James Akerman
Patricia Akre
Linda Aylward
Caitlin Baucom
James Barisano
Lawrence Benaquist
Lynn Brigner
Tim Brooks
Robert Burgess
Louis Ciercielli
Pam Clark
Steve Cosca
Dianne Curry
Debra Dearborn
Betsy Dickinson
David A. Donahue
Kathleen Dow
Barbara Doyle-Wilch
Cecil Elder
Susan Ewers

Kricket Fellows
Lois Ford
Gordon Fournier, II
Mike Freeman, K.B. Slocum Books
John Froats
Edward Gable
Chris Gentry
Sherrain Glenn
George Hansen
Leigh Harralson
Mark Harvey
Mark Heideman
John Henberg
Mellie Humphries
Karl S. Kabelac
Deke Kastner
Joyce Kelley
Dawn Duncan Kendall
Jean Kobeski
Laura Kotsis
Wendy Lauman
Larissa Lorian
Lori Major
Jesse Markow
Richard Markow
Stuart McDougall
Peter Miller
Chris Millspaugh
Venece Moffitt
Alison Moore
Eileen Kennedy Morales
Paula Murphy
Carol Murray
Cindy Ossello
Roger Petrilli
Jack Pratt

Carl and Norma Pullen
Virginia Putnam
Hans Raum
Deirdre Routt
Anne Salsich
Janice Savage
David Schaye
Robbi Seigel
Dixie Server
Nancy Sherbert
Tom Sherry
Bill Slaughter
Adrienne Sockwell
Fay Stahl
Ed Stanchak
Yolanda Theunissen
Tole's Variety
Dawn Troutman
Mike Urritia
Phil Vermillion
Jay Vestal and Family
Chad Wall
Don Wickman

NATIONAL PUBLICITY
DAN KLORES
COMMUNICATIONS

PRODUCED IN ASSOCIATION WITH
WETA WASHINGTON, DC

**EXECUTIVE IN CHARGE OF
PRODUCTION FOR WETA**
DALTON DELAN

PROJECT DIRECTOR FOR WETA
DAVID S. THOMPSON

ASSOCIATE PRODUCER FOR WETA
KAREN KENTON

PUBLICITY FOR WETA
DEWEY BLANTON

SHARON ROCKEFELLER,
President & CEO

———————

A Production of Florentine Films

EXECUTIVE PRODUCER
KEN BURNS

© 2003, The American Lives II
Film Project, Inc.
All Rights Reserved

FUNDING PROVIDED BY
General Motors Corporation
Public Broadcasting Service
Corporation for Public Broadcasting
The Arthur Vining Davis
Foundations
Park Foundation

A NOTE ABOUT THE AUTHORS

DAYTON DUNCAN, writer and producer of *Horatio's Drive,* is the author of seven other books about American history, including *Out West: A Journey Through Lewis and Clark's America,* in which he retraced the route of the expedition. He has been involved with Ken Burns's documentaries for more than a decade and was co-writer and consulting producer of *The West,* the writer and producer of *Lewis & Clark: The Journey of the Corps of Discovery,* and co-writer and producer of *Mark Twain.* He and Burns are now collaborating on a major documentary series about the national parks. He lives in Walpole, New Hampshire.

KEN BURNS, director and producer of *Horatio's Drive,* has been making award-winning documentary films for more than twenty years. He was director of the landmark PBS series *The Civil War, Baseball,* and *Jazz* and executive producer of *The West.* His other films include the Academy Award–nominated *Brooklyn Bridge; The Shakers; The Statue of Liberty* (also nominated for an Oscar); *Huey Long; Thomas Hart Benton; The Congress; Empire of the Air; Thomas Jefferson; Lewis & Clark; Frank Lloyd Wright; Not for Ourselves Alone: The Story of Elizabeth Cady Stanton and Susan B. Anthony;* and *Mark Twain.* His next documentary will be a biography of the prizefighter Jack Johnson. He lives in Walpole, New Hampshire.

A NOTE ON THE TYPE

This book was set in Caledonia, a face designed by
W. A. Dwiggins (1880–1956) for the Mergenthaler Linotype Company in 1939.
It belongs to the family of types referred to by printers as "modern,"
a term used to mark the change in type styles that occurred around 1800.

Separations by North Market Street Graphics, Lancaster, Pennsylvania
Printed and bound by R. R. Donnelly and Sons, Willard, Ohio
Designed by Wendy Byrne